EAST COAST
AUSTRALIA

Sarah Reid, Cristian Bonetto,
Caoimhe Hanrahan-Lawrence, Trent Holden,
Phillip Tang, Jessica Wynne Lockhart

Meet our writers

Sarah Reid
@ @ecotravelist

Editor, author and sustainable travel expert, Sarah has a passion for positive-impact global travel. After travelling to more than 120 countries pre-pandemic, she has recently enjoyed spending time a little closer to home in Arakwal Bundjalung Country (p84).

Cristian Bonetto
@ @rexcat75

Melbourne-born Cristian is as passionate about his home town as he is about his espressos. Indeed, his favourite experience is wandering through Melbourne's laneways (p137) from Flinders St to the State Library, coffee in hand, wintry skies above.

Caoimhe Hanrahan-Lawrence

Caoimhe is a Wiradjuri writer from rural New South Wales, currently living in Sydney on Wangal-Eora land. They can't pass up a regional museum (with the Eden Killer Whale Museum, p115, a case in point) and have a penchant for overnight bus trips.

Trent Holden
@ @hombreholden

A Geelong-based writer, Trent has a fondness for megacities – the more chaotic the better. On the flip side, he's equally happy among remote wilderness areas and national parks, with Victoria's rugged coastline (p162) a favourite hiking destination.

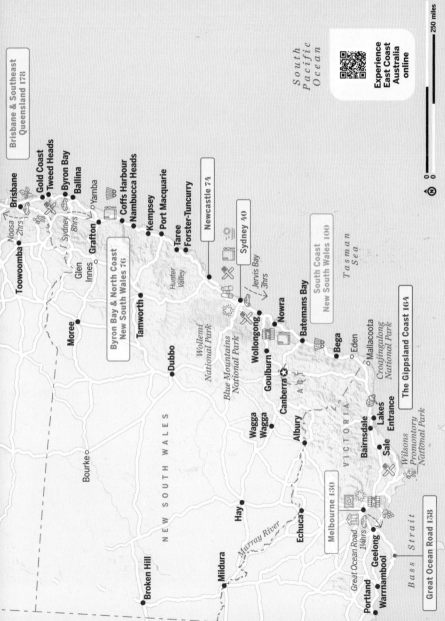

Brisbane & Southeast
Queensland 178

Byron Bay & North Coast
New South Wales 76

Newcastle 74

Sydney 40

South Coast
New South Wales 100

The Gippsland Coast 164

Melbourne 130

Great Ocean Road 138

Experience
East Coast
Australia
online

South Pacific Ocean

Tasman Sea

Bass Strait

Brisbane
Gold Coast
Tweed Heads
Byron Bay
Ballina
Yamba
Coffs Harbour
Nambucca Heads
Kempsey
Port Macquarie
Taree
Forster-Tuncurry
Grafton
Toowoomba
Noosa 2hrs
Sydney 8hrs
Glen
Innes
Moree
Bourke

Tamworth
Dubbo
Wollemi National Park
Hunter Valley
Blue Mountains National Park
Wollongong
Goulburn
Canberra
Nowra
Jervis Bay 3hrs
Batemans Bay
Bega
Eden
Mallacoota
Croajingalong National Park

NEW SOUTH WALES
A.C.T.
VICTORIA

Hay
Wagga Wagga
Albury
Echuca
Murray River
Mildura
Broken Hill

Bairnsdale
Lakes Entrance
Sale
Wilsons Promontory National Park
Great Ocean Road 14hrs
Geelong
Warrnambool
Portland

500 km
250 miles
N
0
0

Immerse yourself in ancient rainforests. Discover the sustainability secrets of the world's oldest living cultures. Feast on fresh seasonal seafood paired with sophisticated local wines. Marvel at the biodiversity of blockbuster marine ecosystems. Sip barista-made coffee while exploring laneway street art. Spot native wildlife on a hike to a lush waterfall. Learn the stories behind architectural icons. Camp on an island. Enjoy a remote beach all to yourself – and perhaps see a kangaroo or two.

This is East Coast Australia.

**TURN THE PAGE AND START PLANNING
YOUR NEXT BEST TRIP →**

South Pacific Ocean

Coral Sea

Great Barrier Reef 232

Cairns & the Queensland Coast 206

Whitsunday Islands

Conway National Park

Eungella National Park

Cooktown

Cape Tribulation

Daintree National Park

Port Douglas

Cairns

Brisbane 24hrs

Innisfail

Tully

Hinchinbrook Island

Ingham

Magnetic Island

Townsville

Charters Towers

Hughenden

Ayr

Bowen

Proserpine

Mackay

Emerald

Barcaldine

Winton

Cloncurry

Normanton

Rockhampton

Gladstone

Biloela

Miles

Bundaberg

Fraser Island

Hervey Bay

Rainbow Beach

Maryborough

Gympie

Noosa

Maroochydore

Charleville

QUEENSLAND

Federation Square (p146), Melbourne

Phillip Tang
@ *@mrtangtangtang*

Phillip Tang grew up in Sydney before calling London and Mexico City home, but the raucous caucus of rainbow lorikeets (p64) in jacaranda trees always summons him back. Besides, Sydney is like the Greatest Culinary Hits of Asia (p50).

Jessica Wynne Lockhart
@ *@WynneLockhart*

An award-winning Canadian journalist, Jessica lives and works in the Queensland village of Mapleton (p202). Her favourite experience is paddling in Booloumba Creek (p199). 'It's tricky to access, but the intrepid are rewarded with the clearest blue water.'

Contents

REINHARD DIRSCHERL/GETTY IMAGES ©

Scuba diver, Coral Sea

Acknowledgement of Country

Lonely Planet would like to acknowledge all Aboriginal nations throughout this country, who have nurtured and maintained the land since time immemorial. This guide was written on, and is written about, the lands of many diverse nations.

We recognise the unique and ongoing connection that Aboriginal peoples have to land and waters and thank them for their efforts to preserve them. We pay our respects to Elders past and present and extend this respect to any Aboriginal or Torres Strait Islander people who may be reading this guide.

We also recognise the ongoing efforts of Aboriginal peoples for reconciliation, justice, and social, cultural and economic self-determination. Sovereignty was never ceded. Australia always was, and always will be, Aboriginal land.

Cultural Sensitivity Warning

Aboriginal and Torres Strait Islander readers are advised that this guide may contain names and images of people who have since passed away.

FIRST NATIONS STATS

Australia's East Coast is home to more than 40 Indigenous nations.

The largest populations of Indigenous Australians live in New South Wales and Queensland (60.1%).

Eleven percent of Indigenous Australians speak a traditional language at home.

INDIGENOUS
CULTURE

Aboriginal and Torres Strait Islander peoples maintain a strong and continuing connection to their Country (traditional lands) stretching all the way along Australia's East Coast, making it one of the best places in Australia to connect with the world's oldest living cultures through arts, food and an excellent range of Indigenous-led tourism experiences.

→ WHOSE COUNTRY?

Learning about whose Country you're visiting adds a rich layer to your experience. Each Aboriginal and Torres Strait Islander group has its own culture, customs, lore and dialect.

▶ Discover more about Australia's First Nations People on p126.

Left Kuku Yalanji man applying ochre markings **Right** Kuku Yalanji guide **Below** Big Esso (p147), Melbourne

URBAN CULTURE

Superb Indigenous galleries, museums and cultural centres can be found in East Coast cities, along with urban bush-tucker walks and innovative and authentic Indigenous-focussed experiences.

↑ INDIGENOUS DINING

Indigenous chefs are making their mark on Australia's culinary scene. Torres Strait Islander chef Nornie Bero's lauded Melbourne restaurant-bar Big Esso (p147) translates Indigenous flavours for the modern palate.

Best Indigenous Culture Experiences

▶ **Explore Queensland's Daintree Rainforest with a Kuku Yalanji guide.** (p224)

▶ **Go on a cultural stand-up paddleboarding adventure on the Coffs Coast.** (p89)

▶ **Take an Aboriginal tour of Sydney Harbour on a Tribal Warrior boat cruise.** (p56)

▶ **Immerse in the Aboriginal culture of the NSW South Coast on a Yuin retreat.** (p124)

▶ **Discover the Aboriginal art, culture and stories of Naarm (Melbourne).** (p146)

FUN FACTS

The Great Barrier Reef is home to more than 600 coral species.

There are 35 artificial ocean pools in Sydney, carved out of the rock face.

Humpback whales travel up to 10,000km on their annual migration from Antarctica to the East Coast.

AQUATIC
ESCAPADES

■■■■ With more than 100 beaches in Sydney alone, Australia's East Coast was made for fun in, on and around the water. From snorkelling on the Great Barrier Reef to surfing the legendary point breaks of NSW to chasing waterfalls in coastal forests and watching whales frolic along the coast, the region is ripe for aquatic pleasures. Get ready to dive in!

→ WHALE WATCHING

Each year between May and November, thousands of humpback whales migrate along the East Coast from their Southern Ocean feeding grounds to mate and calve in warmer waters.

Left Divers, Great Barrier Reef
Right Humpback whale, Hervey Bay
Below Lifesaver on duty

GREAT BARRIER BEAUTY

The world's largest living organism may be under threat, but Queensland's marine icon is still an incredible sight. Take a day trip or stay overnight on an island or a floating pontoon.

▶ Visit the Reef from Townsville (p220) or Cairns (p223).

Best Aquatic Experiences

▶ **Dive into the glorious Great Barrier Reef.** (p232)

▶ **Paddle in waterfalls and idyllic freshwater waterholes in Queensland and beyond.** (p212)

▶ **Surf Byron Bay's famous waves – or learn to.** (p82)

▶ **Scuba dive with placid grey nurse sharks off the north coast of NSW.** (p94)

▶ **Take a boat trip to the mysterious Skull Rock at Gippsland's Wilsons Promontory.** (p173)

↑ LIFE'S A BEACH

There are hundreds – if not thousands – of sandy havens to discover along Australia's East Coast. Stick to lifeguard-patrolled beaches wherever possible, and always check for croc and stinger warning signs.

▶ See p60 for the low-down on Sydney's beaches.

EPIC HIKES
& WALKS

You can hike between ancient rainforest trees, along wild coastal trails and deep in the Aussie bush on Australia's East Coast, with hundreds of trails to choose from, including accessible options. Even short walks require a degree of preparation; check national-park websites for tips.

Cape Tribulation
Accessible Daintree wanders

Three of the four short but beautiful boardwalks in the heart of Queensland's Daintree Rainforest are wheelchair accessible. Weaving through a lush mangrove habitat, the Madja Boardwalk (1.2km circuit/45 minutes) is a particularly mesmerising meander. Look for fish, crabs, and maybe even a saltie below.

🚗 90min drive from Cairns
▶ p212

NORTHERN
TERRITORY

WESTERN
AUSTRALIA

SOUTH
AUSTRALIA

Kalgoorlie-
Boulder

*Great
Australian
Bight*

Port
Augusta

Esperance

Adelaide

Great Ocean Walk
Leave the road behind

Bus from Melbourne to Apollo Bay and explore Victoria's Great Ocean Road slowly on this blockbuster route (110km one way/six to eight days), ending at the iconic Twelve Apostles. Camp on the trail or stay nearby, or sample sections of the trail on invigorating day hikes.

🚗 3hr drive from Melbourne ▶ p162

Warrnambool

Coral
Sea

● Cairns

QUEENSLAND

● Townsville

South
Pacific
Ocean

● Mackay

K'gari (Fraser Island)
Wild walks galore
There are more than 40 marked
trails on the world's largest sand
island. Pack a picnic and follow
the Lake Wabby Walk (8.2km
return/three to four hours)
through the rainforest to the
track's namesake, where you can
enjoy a dip before scrambling up
a sand blow to a great lookout.

🚗 20min drive from Hervey
Bay plus a 30min ferry ▶ p238

● Rockhampton

● Bundaberg

Gondwana Rainforests
Hike to waterfalls
Stretching from southeast
Queensland down to Newcastle,
the Unesco-listed Gondwana
Rainforests are criss-crossed
with walking trails. Love waterfalls? Try the Crystal Showers
Walk (4.4km return/90 minutes)
in Dorrigo National Park.

🚗 1hr drive from Coffs
Harbour ▶ p90

● BRISBANE
● Gold Coast

Blue Mountains
Aboriginal rock art
Near Glenbrook, the Red Hands
Cave Walking Track (8km loop/two
hours) offers a rich taste of Blue
Mountains hiking. The trail winds
through bushland to one of the
most impressive Aboriginal stencil
galleries in the Sydney Basin.

🚗 1hr drive from Sydney ▶ p70

● Coffs
Harbour
● Port Macquarie

● Dubbo

N E W
S O U T H
W A L E S

● Mildura

● Newcastle
● Sydney

● Wagga
Wagga

⚹ Canberra

A U S T R A L I A N
C A P I T A L
T E R R I T O R Y

Tasman
Sea

Wilsons Promontory
Southern Prom highlight
Among the most memorable of the
Gippsland national park's walks is the
20km trek to mainland Australia's most
southerly lighthouse, built in 1859.

🚗 3hr drive from Melbourne ▶ p172

● Bendigo

V I C T O R I A
● Melbourne
● Geelong

Bass
Strait

NOSH BY NUMBERS

Twenty-five percent of Australia's fresh produce is grown in Bundaberg, Queensland.

Around 106 million oysters are produced annually in NSW.

There are more than 2000 cafes and coffee shops in Melbourne.

COASTAL
CUISINE

From the farm-fresh produce of Bundaberg to the plump oysters of the New South Wales coast and the fine wines of the Mornington Peninsula, Australia's East Coast is an epicurean delight. Discover lauded regional restaurants redefining modern Australian fine dining, kick back in cool cafes offering much more than avo on toast, feast on fresh seafood straight off the trawlers, and explore the vibrant multicultural culinary scenes of Sydney and Melbourne.

→ BUSH TUCKER

Look out for East Coast staples including lemon myrtle, warrigal greens and saltbush on restaurant menus, or join an Indigenous tour to learn about traditional uses for native plants.

▶ For more bush-tucker staples see p196.

Left Cafe lunch, Melbourne **Right** Grass-fed beef with warrigal greens **Below** Freshly shucked oysters

TIPPING TIPS

It's customary to leave some small change in the tip jar for a cafe meal. Tip 10% to 15% for good service at restaurants.

↑ ZERO-FOOD-MILE TREATS

From buckets of berries to trays of oysters, many East Coast producers sell fresh food directly from their farms; look out for signs and roadside stalls.

Best Coastal Culinary Experiences

▶ **Stock up at the farm gates of the Bundaberg food bowl.** (p226)

▶ **Eat your way around the coastal fine diners of the NSW Northern Rivers.** (p80)

▶ **Enjoy a Mod Oz lunch one day and yum cha brunch the next in cosmopolitan Sydney.** (p50)

▶ **Slurp fresh oysters on the South Coast of NSW.** (p112)

▶ **Fill your picnic hamper at historic South Melbourne Market.** (p148)

↘ KOALA COUNTRY

Koalas are native to the eucalypt forests of eastern Australia, making it the only place you can observe the iconic marsupials in the wild – a heart-melting experience.

Koalas are easier to spot at dawn and dusk, when they're at their most active.

WILDLIFE
WONDERS

▬▬▬ With two of the world's most biodiverse rainforest systems – the Daintree Rainforest and the Gondwana Rainforests of Australia – among its impressive clutch of globally important habitats, Australia's East Coast brims with native wildlife-watching opportunities. From cassowaries to koalas, many of the region's incredible creatures are found nowhere else on Earth.

Best Wildlife Experiences

▶ Look for cassowaries in Queensland's Wet Tropics World Heritage Area. (p215)

▶ Listen for ancient birds in the Gondwana Rainforests. (p92)

▶ Swim with seals on the NSW South Coast. (p111)

▶ Spot wombats, kangaroos, emus and more on a Wilsons Prom wander. (p172)

↘ SYDNEY HARBOUR BRIDGE CLIMBS

There are four options for climbing Sydney's architectural icon.

For a different perspective on the harbour city, opt for the Burrawa Climb, with an Indigenous storyteller as your guide.

ARCHITECTURE & THE ARTS

▬▬ Whether you prefer to see art hanging in galleries or plastered across laneways, there's plenty of both to be discovered in the cities of the East Coast, with a smattering of excellent regional galleries beyond. Architecture fans will also find much to appreciate, from Sydney's convict-built relics to the opulent buildings of Melbourne that sprang up during the city's post-gold-rush period.

Best Art & Architecture Experiences

▶ Take a backstage tour of the Sydney Opera House. (p47)

▶ Discover the architecture of Melbourne's CBD. (p139)

▶ Tour the recreated studio of a famed artist. (p99)

▶ Purchase meaningful souvenirs at the Cairns Indigenous Art Fair. (p225)

CRAFT DRINKS
& WINE

▬▬▬ A great glass of local wine is never far away on the East Coast, home to 10 wine regions within easy reach of the sea between southeast Queensland and Victoria's Great Ocean Road. Craft breweries are even more abundant, along with an ever-expanding network of distilleries, most with cellar doors. Cheers!

Best Wine & Craft Drinks Experiences

▶ **Pick your favourite craft brewery on the Sunshine Coast.** (p190)

▶ **Enjoy cocktails with harbour views in Sydney.** (p52)

▶ **Get buzzed in Melbourne's coffee and small-bar scenes.** (p143)

▶ **Tour the cellar doors of the Mornington Peninsula and Gippsland.** (p152; p168)

★ **NATURAL WINE**

The natural – also known as minimal-intervention – wine movement, which allows the local terroir to shine, is also big in Australia. Imbibe the trend on the Mornington Peninsula and beyond.

★ **GOING SOFT?**

Booze-free craft bevvies are booming Down Under. Australia's first 'non-alc' bar, Brunswick Aces, opened in Melbourne in 2020; now non-alcoholic brands such as Heaps Normal are becoming the new normal.

Above left Outdoor dining, Sydney **Left** Mornington Peninsula vineyard

ISLAND
TIME

▬▬ Dotted along the East Coast are hundreds of islands with a remarkable diversity of attractions, from dazzling coral reefs to Indigenous culture, luxury glamping to colonial history. Better yet, many of these stunning islands are easily visited on day trips from the coast, while others tempt you to stay a while.

Best Island Experiences

▶ Snorkel just steps from your Great Barrier Reef island eco-hotel. (p232)

▶ Get off-grid on a 4WD K'gari (Fraser Island) trip. (p238)

▶ Swim, camp and whale-watch on Straddie. (p192)

▶ Uncover the convict history of Cockatoo Island. (p55)

▶ Spot koalas on Gippsland's Raymond Island. (p171)

TOP: JOHN CRUX PHOTOGRAPHY/GETTY IMAGES © BOTTOM: CO LEONG/SHUTTERSTOCK ©

EAST COAST AUSTRALIA BEST EXPERIENCES

↑ CASTAWAY CAMPING

It's possible to camp on dozens of East Coast islands, particularly in Queensland. Fitzroy Island is an easy option from Cairns; in the Whitsundays, Scamper (whitsundaycamping.com.au) can rent gear and ferry you to your island of choice.

★ ISLAND DREAMING

From Palm Island (Bwgcolman) in Queensland to NSW's Montague Island (Barunguba), many East Coast isles play pivotal roles in Indigenous culture. Learn more on tours.

Above left Fitzroy Island
Left K'gari (Fraser Island)

Christmas Day, Boxing Day, New Year's Day and 26 January are public holidays. Shops may be closed as people celebrate.

← Sydney New Year's Eve Fireworks

At 9pm and midnight, Sydney Harbour is lit up with several tonnes of dazzling fireworks.

▶ sydneynewyearseve.com

↙ Australian Open

Tennis fans descend on Melbourne in January for the first tennis Grand Slam event of the year.

▶ ausopen.com

Woodford Folk Festival

The 500-acre property of Woodfordia is transformed for the last six days of the year, hosting music, theatre, comedy and more.

▶ woodfordfolkfestival.com

DECEMBER

Australian summers are often very humid.

JANUARY

East Coast Australia in
SUMMER

The heat attracts spiders and snakes. Take care when bush-walking, and check your shoes before putting them on to avoid a surprise.

↘ Stomping of the Grapes

This February festival celebrates the beginning of grape harvesting in the South Coast region.

▶ crookedriverwines. com/events/ stomping-of-the-grapes

↑ Lunar New Year

Australia's large Chinese community celebrates the Lunar New Year with events up and down the East Coast.

FEBRUARY

Rain is not uncommon in summer, especially in the tropics.

This is bushfire season, and some regional areas will be affected by fires.

Demand for accommodation peaks during December and January. Book tours and overnight adventures in advance.

▶ lonelyplanet.com/australia/activities

 Packing notes

Wear light, breathable fabrics and high-SPF sunscreen, and keep a water bottle handy.

EAST COAST AUSTRALIA PLAN BY SEASON

→ Sydney Mardi Gras

Sydney celebrates the strength and diversity of the LGBTIQ+ community in late February or early March with public events and the famed parade.

▶ mardigras.org.au

Sunshine Coast Craft Beer & Cider Festival

Pick from over 100 great Aussie craft brews and catch some live music over three days in mid-March.

📍 Sunshine Coast, p190

▶ craftbeersunshine coast.com.au

← Noosa Festival of Surfing

In early March, celebrate surf culture and watch competitions, including the world's largest surfing-dog competition.

▶ noosafestivalof surfing.com

↙ Melbourne International Comedy Festival

Australian and international comedians converge on Melbourne for this celebrated comedy festival from late March.

▶ comedyfestival. com.au

MARCH

Queensland and northern NSW remain wet and humid.

APRIL

East Coast Australia in
AUTUMN

↘ Sydney Royal Easter Show

Australia's largest annual event, the Easter Show offers amusement rides, a fair and agricultural events.

▶ eastershow.com.au

Byron Bay Bluesfest

Over the Easter long weekend, Byron Bay showcases the best contemporary blues and roots music.

▶ bluesfest.com.au

Good Friday and Easter Monday are public holidays. This four-day weekend is a popular time to travel and visit family.

↗ Anzac Day

On 25 April Australians commemorate the service of Australian and New Zealand troops. It is a public holiday.

MAY

It begins to cool down, though days are usually sunny.

The southern regions are colder than the rest of the country.

🧳 Packing notes

Swap the umbrella for a raincoat, and layer up for variable weather.

Winter is tourism low season, so you will likely avoid large crowds and score some bargains on travel and accommodation.

Laura Quinkan Dance Festival

More than 25 Indigenous troupes from Cape York gather in early July to compete in contemporary and traditional dance.

▶ lauraquinkanfestival.com.au

↗ VIVID Sydney

Sydney is at its most colourful during VIVID, with landmarks transforming through light projections from late May to mid-June.

▶ vividsydney.com

→ Naidoc Week

Across the country, the first full week in July is dedicated to honouring Australia's Indigenous peoples.

JUNE

Winter is usually dry, though some areas experience rainfall.

JULY

East Coast Australia in
WINTER

Quandamooka Festival

From June to September, the Quandamooka peoples from Minjerribah (North Stradbroke Island) share their rich culture.

▶ quandamookafestival.com.au

← Splendour in the Grass

One of Australia's biggest music festivals, Byron Bay's three-day celebration of popular music is held in late July.

▶ splendourinthegrass.com

↑ Hamilton Island Race Week

This week-long yacht race in late August skirts the Great Barrier Reef.

▶ hamiltonislandraceweek.com.au

Pop Up North Queensland

PUNQ takes place every odd-numbered year from late July, showcasing contemporary visual, immersive and performance art.

▶ umbrella.org.au/punq

AUGUST

Days are cooler, but sunburn is still a risk; continue to use sunscreen.

Temperatures drop at night, with morning frosts in the south.

EAST COAST AUSTRALIA PLAN BY SEASON

⌷ Packing notes

A jumper and coat are warm enough during the day. Pack warm pyjamas.

Visitor crowds remain smaller during September and October, though school holidays fall between late September and early October.

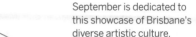

↓ Brisbane Festival

September is dedicated to this showcase of Brisbane's diverse artistic culture.

▶ brisbanefestival.com.au

↗ Cairns Amateurs Racing Carnival

Horse-racing season travels right up to Cairns with this vibrant three-day carnival in early September.

▶ cairnsamateurs.org.au

SEPTEMBER

The days are sunny, making sun safety a must.

OCTOBER

East Coast Australia in
SPRING

↘ AFL Grand Final

Cheer for your favourite team during the final match of the Australian Rules football season in late September.

▶ afl.org.au

Brisbane International Film Festival

This 11-day celebration of the films that have shaped us falls in late October.

▶ biff.com.au

Melbourne Cup

The race that stops the nation: events occur Australia-wide to commemorate the famous horse race in early November.

▶ vrc.com.au

↓ Sculpture by the Sea

From late October Sydney's Bondi Beach hosts this free exhibition featuring sculptures along its 2km coastal walk.

▶ sculpturebythesea.com

EAST COAST AUSTRALIA PLAN BY SEASON

NOVEMBER

Evenings are cool, perfect for outdoor dining.

Rain and humidity ease up in the north.

Though the days are comfortably warm, the seas remain cool. Prepare for a slight shock if you go for a dip.

🎒 Packing notes

Have a broad-brimmed hat for daytime, and a light jacket for after dark.

SYDNEY & SOUTH COAST NSW
Trip Builder

TAKE YOUR PICK OF MUST-SEES AND HIDDEN GEMS

███ From its iconic architecture to its glittering harbour, it's easy to be entranced by Sydney. When you've filled up on glitz and gourmet, head out to the Blue Mountains for a memorable hike, or pack the car for a scenic South Coast road trip.

🗺 Trip Notes

Hub towns Sydney, Wollongong

How long Allow around two weeks

Getting around Use buses, trains, ferries and the light-rail network to get around Sydney, then hire a car for a South Coast road trip. It's two hours by train from Sydney to Katoomba, in the heart of the Blue Mountains.

Tip Parts of some South Coast national parks remain closed for repairs following Australia's devastating 2019–20 bushfires. Check park websites for the latest updates.

COUTTANG/SHUTTERSTOCK ©. POMINOZ/SHUTTERSTOCK ©.
MARI_MAY/SHUTTERSTOCK ©

Blue Mountains
Head for the Unesco-listed mountains west of Sydney for world-class hiking, faded art deco glamour, and antique shopping galore.
🚗 2hrs from Sydney

Jervis Bay & Shoalhaven
Paddle in coastal lakes, sip fine chardonnay, verdelho and chambourcin at friendly cellar doors, and bask in the crystalline blues of Jervis Bay.
🚗 2½hrs from Sydney

⊗ CANBERRA

Kosciuszko National Park

A C T

Eurobodalla
Sample freshly shucked oysters, nibble artisan cheeses, explore pioneer history, and swim, surf or wander along beautiful beaches fringed by national parks in this gorgeous section of the South Coast.
🚗 4hrs from Sydney

N E W
S O U T H
W A L E S

V I C T O R I A

Blue Mountains National Park

Sydney
Step back into history, then down into the underground after-dark scene of the NSW capital, where you can also eat your way around the world without leaving the city.
✈ *1½hrs from Melbourne*

Royal National Park
Discover the many draws of this iconic national park, from the Aboriginal rock carvings near Bundeena to its wild walks, surprising rock formations and blissful beaches.
🚗 *1hr from Sydney*

Wollongong
Lake Illawarra

Goulburn

Morton National Park

Nowra

S H O A L H A V E N

Jervis Bay

○Ulladulla

U R O B O D A L L A

Deua National Park

Batemans Bay
○Mogo

Moruya○

Bodalla○

○Narooma

adbilliga ational ark

○Central Tilba

○Bermagui

Illawarra
Go searching for urban glow-worms, learn about sustainable agriculture on a tasty farm tour, discover an unexpected slice of serenity near Wollongong and feel the power of the ocean at an explosive natural attraction, all just a short hop from the state capital.
🚗 *1½hrs from Sydney*

Tasman Sea

South Pacific Ocean

Bega
○Tathra

○Merimbula

A P P H I R E
C O A S T

○Eden

Sapphire Coast
Go diving and hiking, fossick for gold, and learn about the region's intriguing whale story at the southern end of the South Coast, where the deep blue sea glitters like a precious gem.
🚗 *5hrs from Sydney*

Mallacoota

0 — 100 km
0 — 50 miles

NSW NORTHERN RIVERS
Trip Builder

TAKE YOUR PICK OF MUST-SEES AND HIDDEN GEMS

▬▬ Beautiful beaches and atmospheric towns dot the entire North Coast of NSW, its northern tip particularly well known for its acclaimed restaurants, cool cafes and watering holes, hip boutique hotels and wellness options galore.

🗺 Trip Notes

Hub towns Byron Bay, Kingscliff

How long Allow at least a week

Getting around Hiring a car, ideally at Ballina Byron Gateway Airport or Gold Coast Airport, is the best way to explore beyond central Byron Bay, though there are some wildlife- and culinary-based tour options.

Tip Book accommodation and popular restaurants well ahead, particularly during school holidays and festival periods.

Tweed Hinterland

Driving this farming region's winding country roads is an experience in itself. You'll find farm gates, restaurants, cafes, a top distillery and a renowned Murwillumbah gallery.

🚗 *20mins from Gold Coast Airport*

Nightcap National Park

Part of the Gondwana Rainforests of Australia, this dramatic national park has brand-new visitor facilities, including a new lookout perched above 100m-high Minyon Falls.

🚗 *45mins from Byron Bay*

Clarence Coast

Surf uncrowded waves, pitch a tent by the beach, and feast on fresh prawns straight off the trawlers before heading back up the coast, or down to Sydney.

🚗 *1hr 15mins from Byron Bay*

Gold Coast
• Surfers Paradise

QUEENSLAND

Tweed Heads

○ Kingscliff

Cabarita Beach

○ Pottsville Beach

○ Bangalow

Lennox Head

Lismore •

• Casino

● Ballina

○ Yamba

N E W
S O U T H
Grafton   W A L E S

Tweed Coast
Kingscliff is the Tweed's holiday accommodation HQ, with great beaches and eats to be found here, as well as in Casuarina, Cabarita and Pottsville to the south.

🚗 25mins from Gold Coast Airport

Brunswick Heads
The once-sleepy fishing village now has a food scene to be reckoned with. Three holiday parks nestle alongside the idyllic Brunswick River, and there's a great historic pub shaded by poinciana trees.

🚗 15mins from Byron Bay

Byron Bay
Watch the sun rise from Australia's most easterly point before working your way around the popular holiday town's famous beaches and hot-ticket eateries.

🚗 30mins from Ballina Byron Gateway Airport

Lennox Head & East Ballina
Enjoy leisurely coastal walks and linger in cafes and pubs overlooking the Pacific Ocean in this low-key corner of the Northern Rivers.

🚗 25mins from Ballina Byron Gateway Airport

Byron Bay Hinterland
Dotted with Federation buildings, many of them housing cafes, restaurants and boutiques, the hinterland villages of Bangalow, Newrybar, Federal and Mullumbimby have become destinations in their own right.

🚗 15mins from Byron Bay

South Pacific Ocean

⬆ N

0 ————————— 50 km
0 ————————— 25 miles

MELBOURNE & COASTAL VICTORIA
Trip Builder

TAKE YOUR PICK OF MUST-SEES AND HIDDEN GEMS

▬▬▬ Enjoy the artistic and culinary delights of Melbourne, then venture beyond the big smoke to discover awesome outdoor adventures, laid-back beach towns and, yes, more great food and craft drinks along Victoria's southeastern coastline.

🗺 Trip Notes

Hub town Melbourne

How long Allow 10 to 14 days

Getting around Melbourne has an efficient public-transport network, with connections to the Mornington Peninsula, Gippsland and the Great Ocean Road, though it's more convenient to have a car to explore beyond the city.

Tip While it's generally warm enough for a heart-starting ocean dip in southern NSW in winter, Victoria's beaches are best enjoyed by swimmers during the summer months.

Swan Hill

NEW SOUTH WALES

●Horsham

Bendigo

Melbourne
Appreciate architecture, seek out street art, feast at some of Australia's best restaurants and explore the vibrant neighbourhoods of the nation's capital of cool.
✈ 1½hrs from Sydney

Gisborne

Geelong

● Warrnambool

Great Otway National Park 🚗 ○Lorne

●Anglesea

Port Campbell 🏕 🏖 ○Apollo Bay

Port Campbell National Park

Great Ocean Road
Soak up sublime coastal views and eat your way through the beach towns of Victoria's most famous driving route, or savour the scenery on the six-day Great Ocean Walk.
🚌 1½hrs from Melbourne

Ⓝ 0 — 100 km
0 — 50 miles

Lakes Entrance
Sign up for a heli-SUP tour or go kayaking with the kids at this popular coastal Gippsland family holiday destination.
🚗 *4hrs from Melbourne*

Mallacoota
Relax on a houseboat (no licence required) or simply soak up the easy-going vibe of this remote East Gippsland beach town.
🚗 *6½hrs from Melbourne*

Great Southern Rail Trail
Get on your bike and tackle this 72km Gippsland cycleway, or veer off the trail to tour the region's cool-climate wineries, distillery doors and breweries.
🚗 *1½hrs from Melbourne*

Wilsons Promontory
Lace your boots for spectacular national-park trails and laze on bone-white beaches lapped by turquoise water while keeping an eye out for native wildlife.
🚗 *4hrs from Melbourne*

Mornington Peninsula
Indulge in the gourmet pleasures of this scenic wine region dotted with cellar doors, great restaurants and cafes. Top off the day with a scenic coastal stroll.
🚗 *1hr from Melbourne*

Canberra

AUSTRALIAN CAPITAL TERRITORY

Echuca

Bright

Omeo

VICTORIA

Orbost

Bairnsdale

Paynesville

Marlo

Croajingolong National Park

Moe Traralgon Sale

Portsea

French Island

Leongatha

Phillip Island

Inverloch

Port Albert

Tasman Sea

Wilsons Promontory National Park

Tidal River

Bass Strait

SOUTHEAST QUEENSLAND
Trip Builder

TAKE YOUR PICK OF MUST-SEES AND HIDDEN GEMS

▬▬▬ Queensland is known as the Sunshine State, but its southeastern corner bags the most sunny days – ideal for bouncing between golden beaches and cool craft breweries, and exploring the lush hinterland regions beyond.

🗺 Trip Notes

Hub towns Brisbane, Gold Coast, Noosa

How long Allow at least a week

Getting around It's easy to navigate central Brisbane and the Gold Coast via public transport, but a car is more convenient for exploring the Sunshine Coast and Gold Coast hinterland regions.

Tip It costs just $6.85 per person per night to camp in Queensland national parks – handy if you're travelling in a camper. You'll usually need to bring your own drinking water.

Sunshine Coast Hinterland
Leave the beach behind for a day or two to camp out in national parks, fill your picnic basket at charming country town markets, tick off a hike or two and maybe even spot an elusive platypus.
🚗 1½hrs from Brisbane

Scenic Rim
Visit a camel farm with a difference, tour wineries and a quirky brewery, and admire exquisite mountain scenery and more in this emerging tourism destination.
🚗 1hr from Brisbane

Noosa

Stroll the seriously scenic Coastal Walk in this postcard-perfect Sunshine Coast holiday hub until you find your perfect beach. Then spend an afternoon exploring the Sunshine Coast's burgeoning craft-beer scene.

🚗 *2hrs from Brisbane*

Noosa Heads

Maroochydore

Caloundra

South Pacific Ocean

ondale
tional Park   Maleny

Woodford

Bribie Island

Brisbane

Top off a day exploring the Queensland capital's excellent museums and galleries with a swim at Southbank or a cool drink by the Brisbane River.

✈ *1½hrs from Sydney*

Moreton Bay

Moreton Island

North Stradbroke Island

Escape to easily accessible Straddie for a day (or more) of whale watching, exploring Aboriginal connections, and beach fun.

🚗, ⛴ *1½hrs from Brisbane*

● Ipswich

North Stradbroke Island

QUEENSLAND

South Stradbroke Island

Gold Coast

Experience the Glitter Strip's transformation from greasy-spoon territory to a seaside city with culinary clout – and some killer cocktail bars.

🚗 *1hr from Brisbane*

Southport

Surfers Paradise

● Beaudesert

Burleigh Heads

Gold Coast Hinterland

Go for a hike in search of waterfalls and glow-worms in the lush, ancient rainforests rising up behind the Gold Coast.

🚗 *45mins from Surfers Paradise*

● Coolangatta

Springbrook National Park

Lamington National Park

NEW
SOUTH
WALES

0   50 km
0   25 miles

TROPICAL NORTH QUEENSLAND
Trip Builder

TAKE YOUR PICK OF MUST-SEES AND HIDDEN GEMS

Cairns is an unmissable stop on any East Coast traveller's itinerary, but the fun doesn't end at this buzzy gateway to the Great Barrier Reef and the Daintree Rainforest, with oodles of attractions dotted all the way along this lush stretch of coastline.

🗺️ Trip Notes

Hub towns Cairns, Port Douglas, Townsville

How long Allow nine to 14 days

Getting around Hire a car at Cairns Airport, or book a tour; most tours include hotel transfers.

Tip The humidity is lower during the June to October dry season, and stinger suits aren't required for marine activities, making this time ideal for outdoor exploration. Visit at the beginning or end of the season to avoid the bulk of the crowds.

Cooktown
Embark on a road trip to historic Cooktown via the storied 4WD-only Bloomfield Track, or via the longer, sealed inland route, which takes roughly the same amount of time.
🚗 4½hrs from Cairns

Port Douglas
Relax poolside at one of the holiday town's many resorts, enjoy long walks (and maybe a swim) at fabulous Four Mile Beach and make the most of the easy access to the Daintree Rainforest's Mossman Gorge.
🚗 1hr from Cairns

Atherton Tablelands
Chase waterfalls, swim in crater lakes, spot quirky wildlife and explore an incredible outdoor museum in the refreshingly cool hills above Cairns.
🚗 1½hrs from Cairns

0   100 km
0   50 miles

Cape Tribulation

Immerse yourself in the heart of the otherworldly Daintree Rainforest on a day (or longer) trip to Cape 'Trib', where the rainforest meets the Great Barrier Reef.

🚗 *2½hrs from Cairns*

Great Barrier Reef

Sign up for an outer-reef day trip for the best snorkelling and diving in the iconic marine park, or enjoy the reef for longer on an overnight experience.

⛴ *1½hrs from Cairns or Port Douglas*

Daintree National Park

Great Barrier Reef

Cairns

Sultry Cairns has been upgraded with flash new hotels and a hip small-bar scene, making the multicultural seaside city a fantastic base for reef and rainforest excursions.

✈ *2¼hrs from Brisbane*

Wooroonooran National Park

Innisfail •

Coral Sea

Tully •

Cassowary Coast

Discover hidden beaches, kick back at relaxed pubs, and look out for the formidable feathered namesake of this laid-back coastal region between Cairns and Townsville.

🚗 *1½hrs from Cairns*

Hinchinbrook Island National Park

Townsville

Go koala-spotting on Magnetic Island, visit a next-level aquarium in Townsville, and sign up for a day trip to snorkel or dive the Coral Greenhouse, part of the region's spectacular Museum of Underwater Art.

🚗 *4½hrs from Cairns*

• **Ingham**

Ayr •

7 Things to Know About
EAST COAST AUSTRALIA

INSIDER TIPS TO HIT THE GROUND RUNNING

1 Most Australians Live Here

Australia's population mostly lives in the eastern states, and almost half the country lives in Sydney, Melbourne or Brisbane. However, even though the majority of Aussies live on the East Coast, there's still plenty of room to breathe. The East Coast is full of friendly, tight-knit small towns and natural expanses where you can be alone with the gum trees.

2 It's Bigger Than You Think!

No, really. It takes around 10 hours to drive from Sydney to Melbourne, and three hours to fly from Melbourne to Cairns. Make sure to check your travel time beforehand. Don't worry, Australians fall into this trap as well: many a local has embarked on a half-hour drive only to arrive an hour later than planned.

▶ For information on Getting Around see p244

3 Local Accents Are Detectable

While regional accents in Australia are less defined than in some other countries, Aussies can usually distinguish between someone from Melbourne and someone from Sydney – and will almost definitely be able to identify someone from Far North Queensland!

4 Coffee Is Serious Business

Australians – especially Sydneysiders and Melburnians – love their coffee. If an Aussie recommends a cafe, they probably know what they're talking about.

5 The Animals Are Rather Special

And they (mostly) won't hurt you. Most of the world's marsupials are found in Australia, and the East Coast is full of creatures you won't find anywhere else on Earth. To name just a few, weedy sea dragons, wobbegong sharks and bandy-bandy snakes are all unique to this slice of the globe.

6 Colloquialisms Are Celebrated

You may think you know English, but sometimes speaking 'Australian' is something entirely different. Australians are known to shorten words, add vowels or change meanings. Here's a quick guide to the many 'o's in Aussie slang:

Ambo An ambulance driver

Arvo An afternoon

Avo Are you getting the hang of it? This is an avocado.

Bottle-o A bottle shop. This term is so common that many pubs will label their attached bottle shop a bottle-o.

Defo Definitely!

Garbo No, not the 1930s actress (far from it). This is a shortened form of 'garbage collector'.

Journo A journalist

Muso A musician

Relo A relative or family member

Servo A petrol station (formerly called a 'service station') or sometimes a convenience store

Smoko A quick break from work. Though the word comes from 'smoke break', a smoko no longer requires a cigarette.

7 Sun Safety Is No Joke

Even when it's overcast, sun-conscious Aussies will tell you to slip, slop, slap: slip on a long-sleeved shirt, slop on some sunscreen and slap on a hat. The sun is harsher here than in most other countries, and sunburn is an all-too-easy way to ruin your holiday.

▶ For more Safe Travel measures see p246

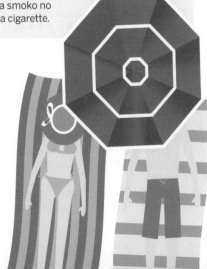

Read, Listen,
Watch & Follow

 READ

Too Much Lip
(Melissa Lukashenko;
2018) An Aboriginal
woman rides a
stolen motorcycle
to visit her dying
grandfather.

**Picnic at Hanging
Rock** (Joan Lindsay;
1967) Haunting
classic about
mysterious school-
girl disappearances.

Dark Emu (Bruce
Pascoe; 2014)
Challenges
assumptions about
Aboriginal culture
before colonisation.

**The Day She
Stole the Sun**
(Cobargo Public
School students;
2020) Depicts the
impact of the 2020
bushfires on the
children of Cobargo.

 LISTEN

**Warm Red Earth
Podcast** Hidden
and often surprising
aspects of
Australian history.

Paul Kelly
Hear his early work
in *Under the Sun*
(1987), enjoy the
more experimental
Life Is Fine (2017)
and delight in his
greatest hits in
*Songs from the
South* (1997).

Baker Boy
Baker Boy's debut
album, *Gela* (2021),
is full of catchy
hip-hop tracks that
blend English with
Yolŋu Matha.

Dr Karl Podcast
Beloved Dr Karl
Kruszelnicki shares
accessible scientific
knowledge.

Courtney Barnett
Barnett's 'sing-speak' vocals shine
in *Sometimes I Sit and Think, and
Sometimes I Just Sit* (2016).

▷ WATCH

Redfern Now (2012–13) Drama series following residents of Sydney's diverse suburb of Redfern.

Playing Beatie Bow (1986) Based on Ruth Park's award-winning novel, this film transports viewers to 1873 Sydney.

The Castle (1997) Typifies Australian humour and full of quotable moments.

Muriel's Wedding (1994; pictured right) Quirky characters trying to escape their small-town lives.

Bluey (2018–) Set in Brisbane, this animated series about a six-year-old blue heeler puppy is a favourite with all ages.

COLLECTION CHRISTOPHEL/ALAMY STOCK PHOTO ©

◎ FOLLOW

@AstroKirsten
Wiradjuri astronomer Kirsten Banks on the Australian night sky.

@GabScanu
Incredible photos of Australia.

@Milligram96
Skits about Australian school life.

@AdrianWidjy
Eating spots in Sydney.

@ChrisHemsworth
Just as charming off-screen.

SYDNEY

BEACH | FOOD | HISTORY

Experience
Sydney
online

SYDNEY
Trip Builder

▬ Listen in on local brunch gossip at a garden cafe, then hike, surf or do sweet, sandy nothing at any of the city's 100-plus beaches. Delight in fusion flavours in Australia's premier multicultural city, then sip drinks with lofty views gazing across the endlessly captivating harbour.

NORTH SYDNEY

WAVERTON

MCMAHONS POINT

Sydney Harbour Bridge

Goat Island

BALMAIN EAST

THE ROCKS

RODD POINT

ROZELLE

Johnstons Bay

Darling Harbour

FIVE DOCK

LILYFIELD

PYRMONT

Glimpse Indigenous art hiking through a national park to **Red Hands Cave** (p67)
🕔 *1 day*

Red Hands Cave (66km)

ANNANDALE

GLEBE

ULTIMO

FOREST LODGE

Admire city views with a cocktail from retro, lofty **Bar 83** (p53)
🕔 *2 hours*

CAMPERDOWN

NEWTOWN

EVELEIGH

WATERLOO

ENMORE

ERSKINEVILLE

Get arty or party with the alternative crowd at **Red Rattler** (p49)
🕔 *3 hours*

MARRICKVILLE

Explore bookable experiences in Sydney online

ST PETERS

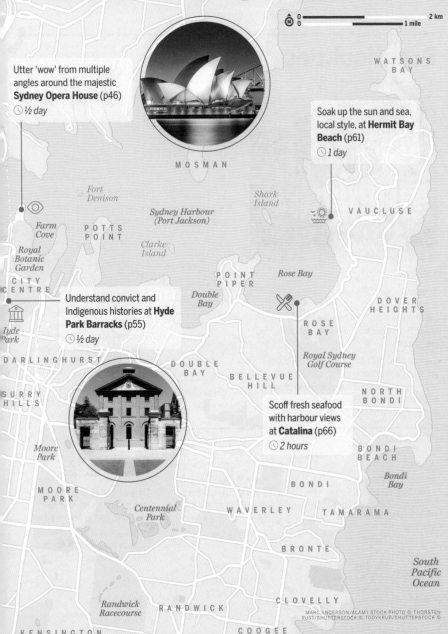

Utter 'wow' from multiple angles around the majestic **Sydney Opera House** (p46)
🕐 ½ day

Soak up the sun and sea, local style, at **Hermit Bay Beach** (p61)
🕐 1 day

Understand convict and Indigenous histories at **Hyde Park Barracks** (p55)
🕐 ½ day

Scoff fresh seafood with harbour views at **Catalina** (p66)
🕐 2 hours

WATSONS BAY

MOSMAN

Fort Denison

Shark Island

VAUCLUSE

Sydney Harbour (Port Jackson)

Farm Cove

POTTS POINT

Clarke Island

Royal Botanic Garden

CITY CENTRE

POINT PIPER

Rose Bay

Double Bay

DOVER HEIGHTS

Hyde Park

ROSE BAY

DARLINGHURST

DOUBLE BAY

Royal Sydney Golf Course

SURRY HILLS

BELLEVUE HILL

NORTH BONDI

Moore Park

BONDI BEACH

MOORE PARK

Bondi Bay

Centennial Park

BONDI

WAVERLEY

TAMARAMA

Randwick Racecourse

RANDWICK

BRONTE

South Pacific Ocean

CLOVELLY

KENSINGTON

COOGEE

0   2 km
0   1 mile

Practicalities

EDINBURGHCITYMOM/SHUTTERSTOCK ©

ARRIVING

Sydney Airport Taxis/airport shuttles to the city cost around $55/25. Trains from beneath the terminal charge a whopping $15.13 each on top of the normal train fare for the short journey into the city.

Central Station Country and interstate trains arrive at Central Station, at the southern end of the city centre. Local trains are downstairs, or head to Railway Sq for buses. Long-distance coaches stop in front of Central Station.

HOW MUCH FOR A

Serve of fish and chips $14

Private surfing lesson $100

Glass of wine $13

GETTING AROUND

Opal Purchase an Opal Card or use the app for all public transport.

Train, bus & light rail Train lines (including new metro lines) radiate from Central Station. Buses are especially useful for reaching the beaches and parts of the inner west. Light rail (tram) is useful for city-hopping in the central business district, and trips to Pyrmont, Glebe, Surry Hills, Moore Park and Randwick.

Ferries Head all around the harbour and up the river to Parramatta. Most people take a ferry to get to Manly in the north because you get the harbour views as a bonus.

WHEN TO GO

DEC–FEB
Peak season coincides with summer school holidays and hot weather

MAR–MAY
Warm but with occasional sudden rain showers

JUN–AUG
Cold nights but regularly sunny days

SEP–NOV
Spring is usually dry and warm

EATING & DRINKING

The city truly celebrates Australia's place on the Pacific Rim, pairing the freshest local ingredients – excellent seafood is a particular highlight – with the flavours of Asia and the Mediterranean. One tradition that has gone global is the easy-going Sydney cafe. The blueprint for this is cafe 'bills' in Darlinghurst, with its large communal table. Here, chef Bill Granger popularised, maybe even invented, smashed avocado on toast (pictured top). Cafes are still good for a solid, often adventurous, meal. The inner west is brimful of them.

Best cocktail wizardry
Eau-de-Vie (p67)

Must-try seafood
Quay (p66; pictured bottom)

CONNECT & FIND YOUR WAY

Wi-fi Free at most accommodation, cafes and shopping centres. A prepaid SIM card for your (unlocked) phone costs around $2; a month of data and unlimited national calls and texts costs $15 to $40.

Navigation Some roads are kilometres long, forking off and changing names; for example, Oxford St starts as Liverpool St and becomes Bondi Rd.

CHEAP FERRIES

Transport on Saturday and Sunday is price capped, so weekends are good for ferry-hopping or out-of-town trips. Problem is, everyone else thinks so too.

WHERE TO STAY

Book ahead around weekends and big events. Prices, even in the budget class, are high.

Neighbourhood	Atmosphere
City Centre	Convenient transport and numerous Asian restaurants, but noisy and with high prices.
Circular Quay & the Rocks	Big-ticket sights, vibrant nightlife and top hotels and restaurants. Made for tourists, with matching high prices.
Newtown & the Inner West	Far from beaches, but bohemian with great cafes and interesting shops. Priced for locals.
Surry Hills & Darlinghurst	Hip eating and drinking precinct and the heart of the gay scene. Hilly with few sights.
Bondi & the Eastern Beaches	Sand, surf and sexy bods. A slow bus ride to the city.
Manly	Beautiful beaches and a privileged community feel, but not much to do in bad weather.

MONEY

ATMs are plentiful, and some charge fewer foreign-transaction fees if you withdraw from a bank that is part of the international ATM network of your bank back home.

01 Sydney Harbour
SCENES

WALKING | VIEWS | FAMILY

▬▬▬ Inspired by yacht sails and surrounded by water, the glorious Sydney Opera House is an iconic symbol of Australia. The building's majestic curves dominate Sydney Harbour and look impressive from every angle. Visitors may be many, but you can still find unique points of view for private gazing at different times of the day.

DAN LÉ/500PX ©

🗺 How to

Getting here There are plenty of trains, buses, ferries and light-rail stops at nearby Circular Quay.

When to go There are fewer visitors on weekdays and after 7pm weekends. Sunsets are always magical.

Cost There is no entrance or entry fee to explore the exterior of the Sydney Opera House or to view the light show.

Circumnavigate the House Not many people know that you can stroll right around the base of the Opera House.

BENNY MARTY/SHUTTERSTOCK ©

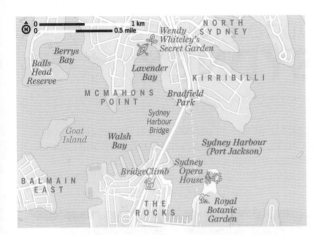

Far left top Sydney Opera House Far left bottom BridgeClimb participants, Sydney Harbour Bridge

Wendy Whiteley's Secret Garden Australian artist Brett Whiteley and his then-wife Wendy built a home at lovely Lavender Bay in 1970. After Brett's death Wendy worked to establish a garden on the difficult, sloping site, and today the expansive space (free and open to visitors) is filled with Australian plants and offers harbour views and a glimpse of the Opera House.

Get the blood pumping Don a headset, a safety cord and a grey jumpsuit for **BridgeClimb**: a guided 3½-hour ascent of Sydney Harbour Bridge that'll give you a white-knuckle view of the Opera House as the wind whips up. The exhilarating climb is best, though priciest, at dawn and dusk. A cheaper 90-minute 'sampler' climb (to a lower point) is also available, as are express climbs via a faster route (2½ hours).

For a quieter perspective, embark on a kayak tour at dawn as the sun kisses the surrounding waters. Departing from places such as Lavender Bay boat ramp, most tours include a guide, all gear and a briefing for novices.

Picnic break Enjoy an alfresco meal under Moreton Bay fig trees on the crowd-free Tarpeian Lawn at the edge of the Royal Botanic Garden, adjacent to the Opera House.

Light show *Badu Gili* is a light show of Aboriginal art projected onto the Opera House at sunset. It's been such a hit that it's become a daily event.

Inside the Opera House

If you fall in love with the Sydney Opera House, or want to, you can take a tour inside for lesser-seen delights.

Peek at the six fine performance spaces that stage around 40 shows a week – and it's not all opera. Modern concerts, theatre and stand-up comedy happen here too, so book ahead for events. The renovated (mid-2022) Concert Hall now features panoramic screens showcasing past performances, and is especially impressive for architecture lovers with its radiant art deco shell design. Some tours take you backstage to see actors rehearsing, or even into a green room for breakfast.

02 Underground SYDNEY

ART | NIGHTLIFE | LGBTIQ+

▬▬▬ Sydney's underground art, party and performance scene sprang up from restrictive drinking laws. Check out edgy galleries during the day, and after the sun sets invite yourself to fringe theatre and places to dance the night away. Rockers, writers, dreamers, community-minded artists and allies all have their own enclaves.

IMPERIAL ERSKINEVILLE ©

🗺 How to

Getting here Parties happen around Redfern and the inner west and are advertised on social-media pages, sometimes with secret locations only revealed on the night.

When to go Art and performance spaces are hot year-round, but book ahead for events around the Gay and Lesbian Mardi Gras.

Cost Party nights and performances are usually ticketed, while bars and pubs cost sweet nothing.

What to wear Check social-media snaps to see what's hot.

FIMINA ANNA/SHUTTERSTOCK ©

Far left top Imperial Erskineville **Far left bottom** Sydney Gay and Lesbian Mardi Gras parade

Bars and pubs To mingle and meet a mix of left-of-centre people, duck into the friendly **Bearded Tit**, a bar owned and run by queer people. The intimate space hosts performance art, events (drag-queen bingo, anyone?) or DJs most nights. **Goros** is an anime-themed restaurant-bar with karaoke, arcade games and a young crowd.

A tiny, unexpected slice of artistic life in stuffy Summer Hill, the **Temperance** bar attracts writers and creatives to its dark Victorian interior to sup locally sourced beer and wine. Live music and poetry have sometimes been spiced up with presentations on topics such as 'Women in electronic-music history'.

The **Duke of Enmore** has become an alternative rock 'n' roll hub in the inner west. Old-skool punk and indie playlists in the candlelit pub attract musos and tattooed friends.

Party nights Regular parties with a carnival of fantastical, gender-bending performances go off at **Honcho Disko** at the Imperial Erskineville. **Heaps Gay** events are magnets for a mixed crowd (the space isn't just gay and lesbian, despite the name), who come for live bands, DJs and death-dropping hype girls. If that still feels too commercial, look up **Bad Dog** (bad dog.net.au), which thinks leather is conservative and prefers to stretch the boundaries of what a queer party should be.

Festivals Look out for Burning Man–inspired festivals **Burning Seed** and **Dragon Dreaming** in country New South Wales.

☼ I Like to Watch

Not in the mood for dancing? At the refurbished **Imperial Erskineville** (of *Priscilla, Queen of the Desert* fame) you can sit down for dinner but still catch a drag show.

Solo travellers who want to mingle should head to **107 Projects**, a huge art collective with exhibition and installation spaces for experimental art, plus workshops. It's easy to strike up a conversation at its bohemian cafe. Sometimes there's speed dating.

Fringe musicians and alternative theatre are under the spotlight at **Red Rattler**. Look out for bent burlesque shows put on by **Burlesk of the Bizarre**.

■ Recommended by Venus Vamp, *Sydney performer, producer, artist and queer witch* @venusvamp

03 Yummy Prawns & YUM CHA

EATING | MULTICULTURAL | DRINKING

Over a third of Sydney's residents were born overseas, and it shows in the city's wealth of dining options. Restaurants range from *pho* noodle joints that evoke a trip to Vietnam to dumpling-cart banquet halls. Persian fine diners serve pomegranate-bejewelled dishes, while Thai-kitsch bistros sell coconut snacks to go. Everything tastes authentic, just with fresh local produce (and fatter prawns).

How to

Getting here All the areas in the CBD are easily walkable from places like Circular Quay.

When to go Book ahead for weekends, and even from midweek in the warmer months.

BYO If you're having more than a couple of drinks, it can be better value to bring your own beer or bottle of wine. Restaurants will state if they're BYO; corkage is usually around $5 per bottle of wine.

CHEDIMA/SHUTTERSTOCK ©

Left Vietnamese *pho* **Far left top** Yum cha selection **Far left bottom** Mango Coco dessert plate

Groups of friends congregate at Korean restaurants such as **Basax** for sticky fried chicken. Casual and cute Thai restaurants line Campbell St, off George St in Haymarket. Sydney's Thai community gossips over desserts at bistros like **Mango Coco** in between shopping for groceries.

The 'food courts' of Dixon and Sussex Sts in Chinatown are actually bustling indoor hawker stands like you might find in Indonesia, Thailand, Singapore and Vietnam. Yum cha is a weekend brunch ritual for the Cantonese community. You can turn up hungry at the red-and-gold banquet halls of Haymarket and nab a bamboo steamer of prawn dumplings right off the trolleys within minutes.

The Lebanese community first called Surry Hills and Redfern home in the 1880s, and that legacy lingers in Persian, Turkish and Middle Eastern restaurants.

The inner-west neighbourhood of Marrickville has a stretch of good Vietnamese restaurants from the train station to Marrickville Rd. It's the real deal, just with updated interiors for the hip crowd.

Newtown is Sydney's plant-based capital, with a dozen vegan Japanese, Vietnamese, Thai, gelato, 'butchery', 'cheese' and dumpling joints on King St. The epicentre is **Gigi Pizzeria**.

A 25-minute express train whizzes you to the other CBD, Parramatta, where cottages in the adjacent Harris Park have become restaurants and dessert diners serving dishes from every region of India.

Best Hidden Asian Diners

Cabramatta's **Battam-bang Restaurant** is a long-time fave with Khmer locals seeking home-style dishes. Try the dry Phnom Penh noodles and a serving of crispy deep-fried intestines.

Grab some sticky rice and take yourself to flavour town with juicy barbecued ox tongue, spiced pork sausages and papaya salad at **Lao Village** in Fairfield. Where have you been all my life?

Hidden between a roadside petrol station and a car wash, little **2 Foodies** in Mt Pritchard has *pho* broth so deep, rich and hearty you'd be lucky to eat one this good even if you grew up in a Vietnamese household.

■ Tips by **Kevin La**, *food blogger and content creator* from southwest Sydney @sydneyfoodboy

04 Bar Crawl with **A VIEW**

DRINKING | VIEWS | HARBOUR

▬▬▬▬ Toast the smashing views of Sydney's harbour, beach and twinkling lights. Drink at giddy heights gazing across the Opera House, or ditch the crowds and kick back in a park with the trees framing the water.

DOUBLE DEUCE LOUNGE ©

🍸 Cocktail Joy

Moya's Juniper Lounge, Redfern Gins galore and live jazz on Sunday.

PS40, CBD Try the hot and cold Africola.

Jangling Jack's, Potts Point Banging classics.

Double Deuce, CBD (pictured) Stellar cocktails and exceptional staff.

Cantina Ok, CBD Ridiculously good agave selection.

🗺 Trip Notes

Getting here After you take a train, bus or light rail to Circular Quay, everything is within stumbling distance. For Bondi, take bus 333 from stand B or a 20-minute Uber.

When to go Summer for long, scorching days; crisp, sunny winter for fewer crowds and no summer downpours.

Alcohol schmalcohol Sydney's non-alcoholic scene is taking off, with local distilleries producing gin, beer and other tipples with all the botanicals and none of the hangovers.

■ Tips by **Chau Tran,** *bartender at Burrow Bar* @burrow_bar, @chaueth

01 **Glenmore Hotel** feels hidden but is extremely popular with those in the know for a boozy lunch. Book ahead for a rooftop seat with views across the harbour and Opera House.

03 Head right to the source: drink outdoors alongside the water around the Opera House and Harbour Bridge at the **Opera Bar**, day or twinkly night.

04 A DIY picnic with bubbly or juice under a tree at the **Royal Botanic Garden** rewards with free views of the Opera House, Australian flora and raucous birdlife.

MOSMAN

WATSONS BAY

Sydney Harbour Bridge

Sydney Harbour (Port Jackson)

Circular Quay

Pitt St

Macquarie St

Royal Botanic Garden

POTTS POINT

The Domain

DARLING POINT

VAUCLUSE

ROSE BAY

Hyde Park

DARLINGHURST

EDGECLIFF

Royal Sydney Golf Course

BELLEVUE HILL

SURRY HILLS

WOOLLAHRA

Cooper Park

Moore Park Rd

Moore Park

Oxford St

Syd Einfeld Dr

BONDI BEACH

BONDI

Bondi Bay

Centennial Park

BONDI JUNCTION

Waverley Park

Bondi Rd

TAMARAMA

South Pacific Ocean

WAVERLEY

Queens Park

02 Sip cocktails using native ingredients from the retro-futuristic velvet lounges at **Bar 83**. On the 83rd floor of Sydney Tower, it's the city's loftiest bar, with wide-angle views across the city and harbour.

05 Sydney microbrewed beer tastes as refreshing as a breeze off adjacent Bondi Beach at **Icebergs Dining Room & Bar**. The iconic blue sea pool is a visual postcard of Sydney.

2 km
1 mile

05 In the Footsteps of
CONVICTS

HISTORY | CULTURE | ARCHITECTURE

▬▬▬▬ Glimpses of what has gone before are everywhere in Sydney. Ancient rock carvings adorn the headlands, convict-hewn roads are still in service, and large chunks of the harbour look much as they did when the First Fleet muscled in and changed absolutely everything else.

How to

Getting here Hyde Park Barracks is outside St James Station, or from Circular Quay it's an interesting 15-minute walk down Macquarie St with its historic buildings.

When to go The city centre can get hectic with office lunchers during the week, making weekends the quieter option.

Discount pass A Sydney Museums Pass gives access to 12 historic properties in and around Sydney.

Convict Sites

Start with the place convicts called home: **Hyde Park Barracks**. Not only were convicts housed here, but convict stonecutters, bricklayers and carpenters built the handsome building that is today a modern museum. A 2020 refurbishment added interactive installations, theatrical events and displays that turn dry history into an exploration of human struggle.

Cockatoo Island was a harsh place of punishment, with the cat-o'-nine-tails and underground solitary cells. As at Hyde Park Barracks, the system here was based on work, and inmates were controlled by a system of bells. Tours of Cockatoo Island (cockatooisland.gov.au) give insights into its history, or you can get a ferry here from Circular Quay and explore.

🌿 Indigenous Plants

While First Fleeters came close to starvation in the early years, local Aboriginal tribes had millennia of knowledge of living off the land. See examples of edible plants harvested by the Gadigal, Dharug and Dharawal peoples in the Cadi Jam Ora (First Encounters) beds of the **Royal Botanic Garden**.

Left Cockatoo Island **Above left** Hyde Park Barracks **Above right** Hyde Park Barracks interior

Aboriginal Sydney

Sydney is the land of the Gadigal people. It is an important place for all Aboriginal people and they wish to tell their own stories of their survival. You can get the 393 bus to La Perouse to go on a number of First Contact walking tours (search for 'First Contact' at nationalparks.nsw.gov.au).

The boat *Tribal Warrior* provides an Aboriginal tour of Sydney Harbour (search for 'cultural cruise' at nationalparks.nsw.gov.au).

The **Australian Museum** has an Aboriginal section run by Aboriginal curators (australian. museum/learn/first-nations).

The Rocks

Known to the Gadigal people as Tallawoladah, Sydney's oldest neighbourhood was the hub of convict- and wharf-trading life in the early 19th century. Today the Rocks is a place of glitzy shops and bars in the shadow of the Harbour Bridge. Colonial marks are still here, though, and they come alive with a tour, but you can

ⓘ Rat Time Capsule

When renovators lifted the floorboards of the convict wards at Hyde Park Barracks in 1979, they discovered a time capsule: convict-era rats had stolen boarders' clothing and other everyday items to fashion their nests. The dry environment under the floor had preserved 120,000 pieces. It's no wonder the nests were so extensive: convicts complained of packs of rats nipping at their faces throughout the night.

Today the barracks display 4000 items from this treasure trove of coins, leather, rosary beads, hammock rope, aprons, bonnets, cotton spools, dresses and brooches. There are even a few rat skeletons!

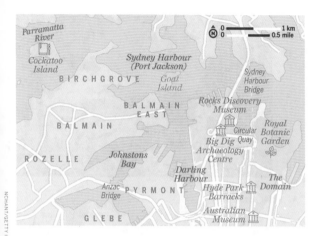

Left Hammocks, Hyde Park Barracks
Below The Rocks Market

easily wander around yourself, time-jumping with lunch in a modern-day cafe or shopping at the outdoor market. Architecture highlights are the sandstone splendour of Sydney Observatory, the brick warehouses of Campbell's Stores, and Sergeant Major's Row of terrace houses.

Archaeological digs have discovered the remains of households, and there are a number of museum sites to visit here, the main one being the **Big Dig Archaeology Centre**. Tucked away down a lane-way, the **Rocks Discovery Museum** digs deep into the area's history on an artefact-rich tour. Sensitive attention is given to the Rocks' original inhabitants, the Gadigal people, and there are interesting tales of early colonial characters.

First Contact

James Cook's monument-marked landing place is on the southern side of the park in Kurnell, 45 minutes south of the CBD. The **Kurnell Visitor Centre** conveys the impact of European arrival on the local Aboriginal people, and has information on the surrounding wetlands and Cook's life and expeditions.

Further out west, several interesting historic houses date from the very earliest days of colonial settlement. Parramatta was founded with First Fleet convict labour when Sydney Cove proved to be lousy for growing veggies.

■ By Paula Jane Byrne
Historian Paula Jane Byrne is a visiting scholar at the State Library of New South Wales and author of Criminal Law and Colonial Subject. ResearchGate @Paula-Jane-Byrne

Life for the First Convicts

SURVIVAL OF THE FITTEST IN SYDNEY TOWN

For the early convicts arriving at present-day Circular Quay, Sydney was a place of control and punishment. The system allowed little ways that convicts could shape their own lives, but it was also fickle, and they could be lashed, imprisoned or re-transported to another part of the NSW coast.

Left Arrival of the First Fleet at Sydney Cove **Middle** Parramatta Female Factory **Right** Convict gang, Sydney

PICTORIAL PRESS LTD/ALAMY STOCK PHOTO ©

Beginnings

The eastern side of Sydney Cove – Warrane in the language of Traditional Owners the Gadigal – is the site of the first permanent European settlement in Australia. It was established on Gadigal country in 1788.

The original shoreline is marked by bronze discs in the pavement. Looking up the hill into the city, imagine two even rows of brick huts, allocated to convicts in 1792.

On the western side of Circular Quay, the Rocks was the commercial area of convict life. Houses were carved up, and lofts, garden space and sheds were rented out in the early 1800s. Convicts exchanged rations, rum and even stolen goods as rent. They raised income from working after hours: after finishing their government work, they were able to hire themselves out as labourers, in a kind of gig economy.

The rum brought into the houses gave landlords ideas, and numerous informal public houses opened up. If you owned one glass or even a cooking pot you were in business.

Tragic Second Fleet

Train your gaze on the centre of Circular Quay and imagine the first wharf here, where convicts landed on arrival. In 1789 the Second Fleet arrived in Warrane and 486 convicts were brought on shore. Many were starving and ill with scurvy, and soon died. Standing here, imagine the shock and horror that day. Some convicts fainted, while others crept upon their knees or were carried on the backs of others.

The convicts had been transported by a merchant slaving company with no interest in keeping their human cargo alive. They would not make any money by selling them, so what was the point in feeding them?

Female & Male Convicts

Each ship was its own little culture that depended on the personality of the captain.

For women this could mean the difference between repeated rape or cohabitation with a sailor or officer, or doing business on board washing clothes or trading in articles bought at ports.

> In 1789 the Second Fleet arrived in Warrane and 486 convicts were brought on shore. Many were starving and ill with scurvy, and soon died.

When female convicts landed after 1813 they were taken up the Parramatta River by boat to the Parramatta Female Factory (parragirls.org.au). You can take the same route by ferry to Parramatta and see the factory.

Male convicts had set work hours, and to be found in the street outside these hours was an offence. Work was in the building industry and the stores, where rations were distributed and produce taken in. When male convicts arrived, they were told to find lodgings for themselves in the squalid Rocks. It was (and is) a maze that resembled an Irish village, with higgledy-piggledy streets and no street numbers so people could not be easily found by the constables.

The English government owned the labour of the convicts, not the convicts themselves. Convicts were sentenced to work for seven or 14 years, or for life. Alternatively, the governor could pardon them, and then they lived as if free. The last convict ship arrived in NSW in 1850 after much opposition to (not sympathy for) the convicts. Anti-convict sentiment formed part of the movement for democracy.

🏛 Convict Labour

Walk through Sydney and imagine the hewn stone, the mortar, the limewash and the cut wood. This labour was extracted from male convicts by fear of the lash. Many convict-made buildings and other constructions are still visible today.

St James' Church 179 King St

Supreme Court building Elizabeth St

Man-O' War steps Near the Botanic Gardens

Parliament House Macquarie St

Mint Museum Macquarie St

Parts of the Sydney Conservatorium of Music Near the Botanic Gardens

National Trust Centre Observatory Hill

Cadmans Cottage The Rocks

Hyde Park Barracks Macquarie St

Argyle Cut The Rocks

06 Let's
BEACH

BEACHES | NATURE | SURFING

Nowhere else does the city kiss the sea so spectacularly. Sydneysiders are blessed with over 100 beaches, each with its own personality. Hidden strands favour sunbathing with a book, and some stretches of dramatic water are known only to surfers.

🗺️ How to

Getting here The eastern beaches can be reached from the city centre by bus. For the north, take a ferry from Circular Quay to Manly.

When to go Sunny weekdays can be quieter, especially in the mornings. Cloudy days see fewer crowds and more locals and surfers.

Life-savers Sydney's surf life-savers watch over certain stretches of major beaches, marked with red-and-yellow flags, where it's safest to swim.

Social Swimming

Clovelly Beach is all concrete, so you can laze back and have a drink or jump straight off the platform into the water. Afterwards, there's a good bowlo (lawn bowls club) uphill for a drink and a game with friends. Plus **Clovelly Bowling & Recreation Club** has the best views over the coast of any bowlo in the world.

Quiet Swimming

Mahon Pool near Maroubra is calm and less busy than most beaches, but with dramatic surf at its edges. At **Little Bay Beach**, south of Malabar, you can't even see any buildings, just the beautiful flat water and outcrops for snorkelling. It's very quiet, with mostly local swimmers. Quiet **Hermit Bay Beach**, at the end of Nielsen Park's walking trails, faces the distant Harbour Bridge. It's ideal for reading

🏖️ Nude Beach

Lady Bay Beach is Australia's oldest nudist beach. It's not just for ladies – gay men, straight couples and international visitors have sought solace in the calm, blue waters in their birthday suits for decades. Shrug off your clothing and the distant city, sheltered by Lady Bay's two rocky natural piers.

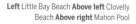

Left Little Bay Beach **Above left** Clovelly Beach **Above right** Mahon Pool

a book on the soft wheatgrass under shady trees. You don't even need to touch the sand; you can launch off a little rock wall into the water. **Shelly Beach** in Manly is protected from wild weather. There are no southerly winds, so you can take in the serenity.

Ocean Pools

If you have young kids or shark paranoia – or the surf just doesn't excite you – you can chill out at one of Sydney's 40 artificial ocean pools, located up and down the coast. Most are free. Some, like **Mahon Pool** and **Bronte Bogey Hole**, are what are known as bogey holes: natural-looking rock pools where you can safely splash about and snorkel, even while the surf surges in. Calm **McIver's Ladies Baths** (also known as Coogee Women's Baths) is open only to women and children; **Fairlight Rock Pool** is similarly quiet and family-friendly. Others, like **MacCallum Pool** and the famous **Bondi**

🏄 Surfing for Beginners

The most important thing at the beginning is just to get out there. Your paddling won't get stronger unless you're in the water all the time. Sydney beaches can get crowded, but don't let that deter you. Focus on getting your own waves.

Stay away from Bondi – it's so busy. Manly is relaxed and best for starting out. It can be quite protected, unlike Bondi and Maroubra, whose aggressive waves can dump you. South Cronulla is a long, more isolated beach with loads of space to find your own stretch.

■ Lucy Small,
surfer and activist
@saltwaterpilgrim

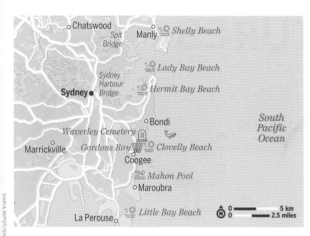

Left Surfer, Cronulla **Below** Bondi to Coogee coastal walk

Icebergs, resemble swimming pools. The ocean pools normally close one day a week so the seaweed can be cleaned out.

Walking & Snorkelling

The most famous beachside walk is the spectacular **Bondi to Coogee**, but there are plenty of trails (walkingcoastalsydney.com.au), with some of the most surprising ones around the harbour. The **Harbour Bridge to Spit Bridge** walk and the **Spit Bridge to Manly** walk are excellent stretches. Or do the 80km **Bondi to Manly** stretch over a few days (bonditomanly.com). One of the best snorkelling spots is **Gordons Bay**, where a free underwater nature trail has been set up, as is **Shelly Beach**, next to Manly.

Whale Watching

Each year, more than 30,000 humpback and southern right whales pass along Sydney's coast between May and November as they migrate between Antarctica and the warmer waters of the Pacific. It's easy to spot their spouts from the cliffs – grab a perch at Waverley Cemetery and keep an eye out for the whale-watching boats.

CREATURES
of Sydney

01 Ibis
Sydney's 'bin chicken' fossicks for food scraps in park bins and is drawn to tourists snacking at Circular Quay.

02 Silver gull
Loves screeching 'kwarwh' and fighting other seagulls for chips at the beach.

03 Laughing kookaburra
The bird emblem of NSW. If you don't hear them in Centennial Park, any other national park is a safe bet.

04 Australian magpie
Swoops from trees at joggers, cyclists and jumpy tourists in Sep-tember (and around) to protect its chicks.

05 Sulphur-crested cockatoo
So rowdy, so Sydney, this parrot rules from Mrs Macquarie's Point to the outer suburbs.

06 Rainbow lorikeet
This parrot flocks for colourful – and noisy – sunset orchestras across Sydney.

07 Flying fox
Look up for another Hyde Park and Centennial Park nightly visitor as this bat, silhouetted against the sky, seeks eucalyptus pollen.

08 Huntsman spider

After summer down-pours, this fist-sized visitor dries off on bedroom walls looking deadly – but it's not.

09 Sydney funnel-web spider

The world's second-most-venomous spider adores Sydney gardens after rain. Relax: no deaths have occurred since an antivenin was devised in 1981.

10 Eastern water dragon

Even lizards love Sydney's water and sun, especially in Lane Cove National Park and the bush around Parsley Bay.

11 Goanna

Look out for this giant, gentle lizard sunbathing along the Manly Scenic Walkway.

12 Brushtail possum

Catch the possum's retro-reflective eyes at night as it scurries around Hyde Park.

13 Brush-turkey

Wanders leafy North Shore suburbs scratch-ing up million-dollar gardens.

Listings

BEST OF THE REST

Sociable Eating

Farmhouse $$

Has a sociable common table where you can dig into simple and scrumptious oysters and cod in now cosmopolitan King's Cross.

Chat Thai $

Reasonably priced, loaded with flavour and constantly buzzing. A go-to for meeting up with friends and family.

Ms G's $$

Not totally Chinese, but loud, brash and delicious fusion food regardless. The mixed bar and communal-warehouse vibe means you'll quickly feel part of the local eating scene.

Seafood & Views

Catalina $$$

Super-fresh seafood and an inventive, varied set menu makes any special occasion sparkle.

Quay $$$

Book weeks ahead for the cutting-edge degustation menu and unforgettable vistas of Sydney Harbour. Ask for a table with an uninterrupted view of the Opera House.

Pilu at Freshwater $$$

Brilliant Sardinian seafood know-how and Italian wines, backing a northern beach. Time your visit for sunset to create a long-lasting Sydney memory.

Ripples Chowder Bay $$$

Elevated terrace with scenic harbour perspectives and punchy salmon and prawn dishes. The port and occasional naval ship in dock will suit those with industrial tastes.

Aussie Fusion

Ester $$$

Sydney's contemporary-casual dining scene without the gimmicks. Don't miss the blood-sausage sandwich or the excellent vegan set menu.

LuMi $$$

Totally delicious blends of Italian and Japanese influences. Degustations are a tour de force.

Rockpool Bar & Grill $$$

A sleek operation famous for its dry-aged, full-blood Wagyu burger (make sure you order a side of the hand-cut fat chips).

Bathers' Pavilion $$$

At Balmoral Beach, the modern French-Aussie seasonal menu focuses on produce from small local providers, with plenty of seafood.

Three Blue Ducks $$

The adventurous chefs at this lunchtime favourite have a strong commitment to using local, organic and seasonal ingredients whenever possible to cook in the charcoal pits.

Section of the Great North Walk

🌿 Nature & First Nations

Great North Walk

Starting at Sydney Harbour, this hike weaves through Lane Cove National Park to the beautiful Berowra Valley Regional Park and into Ku-ring-gai Chase National Park.

Guringai Aboriginal Tours

Also within the national park, this Aboriginal-owned and -operated tour company offers excellent insights into the plentiful cultural heritage spots of the beautiful Ku-ring-gai.

Red Hands Cave

Heading deeper into Ku-ring-gai Chase National Park, the Resolute picnic area has faint Indigenous handprints in ochre at Red Hands Cave. Then, the Resolute Track heads past an Aboriginal engraving site.

Tribal Warrior

Learn about and experience Aboriginal culture and history on this two-hour cruise, stopping at Clark Island for a cultural performance and a guided walk.

Whale Watching Sydney

Humpback and southern right whales habitually shunt up and down the Sydney coastline, sometimes venturing into the harbour. Between mid-May and November, WWS runs two- and three-hour tours.

🍸 Drinking Dens

Eau-de-Vie $$$

Hidden away, but worth tracking down for its cocktail wizardry when you've had enough of the endless sunshine.

Grandma's Bar $$$

Louche and laid-back underground venue with exposed brick serving up potent cocktail concoctions with a side of jaffles (grilled cheese sandwiches).

Humpback whale

CHAMELEONSEYE/SHUTTERSTOCK ©

Lazybones Lounge $$

Head out of the city centre and discover the gloriously mellow vibes and live music at this low-lit Marrickville star.

Uncle Ming's $$

A dark Chinese cave of cinema fantasies lives in this small bar secreted in a basement by a shirt shop. It's an atmospheric spot for leisurely exploration of the cocktail or dumpling menu.

Shady Pines Saloon $$

From the laneway entrance (look for the white door) you'd never guess there was a subterranean honky-tonk bar in urban-boho Darlinghurst. Sip whisky and craft beer amid enormous North American taxidermy.

✨ Free Fun

Art Gallery of NSW

One of the main players of museum life in Sydney, with loads to see in its free sections, including regular concerts, screenings and children's activities. Free guided tours are offered on various themes.

Chau Chak Wing Museum

This latest museum at the University of Sydney exhibits Indigenous cultural objects and Australian, European and Asian art.

White Rabbit

Cutting-edge, contemporary Chinese art (works produced since 2000) that is funny, sexy and idiosyncratic.

Green Spaces & Beaches

Wandering the city's parks, gardens and national parks (though there's a vehicle fee) is gratis, and rolling out your towel on the sand is an Australian birthright.

Sydney Harbour

You can walk over that other great icon, the Sydney Harbour Bridge, and wander through Luna Park (there's a charge for rides).

Historical Buildings

Many of Sydney's most beautiful old buildings are free to enter, including the Customs House, the Mint, St Mary's Cathedral, the State Library and the GPO.

Architectural Gems

Window-shoppers should peruse the exquisite Queen Victoria Building and the Strand Arcade. For more modern architectural thrills, check out Central Park and the nearby Dr Chau Chak Wing Building.

Local Markets

Kirribilli Markets

A wonderful monthly market offering everything from vintage clothes and antiques to kids' gear and all kinds of jewellery.

Surry Hills Markets

There's a chipper community vibe at this monthly market, with mainly locals renting stalls to sell/recycle their old stuff: clothes, CDs, books and sundry junk. Bargains aplenty!

The Grounds Markets

Deep in Alexandria's warehouses, this garden cafe has a great weekend market, with craft jewellery, quirky clothes and tasty baked goods.

Glebe Markets

Dreadlocked inner-city hippies beat a hazy course to this crowded Saturday market. Once massaged and fuelled up on lentil burgers, they retreat to the lawns and chill out to an African-drum soundtrack.

Bondi Markets

The kids are at the beach on Sunday while their school fills up with Bondi groovers rummaging through funky secondhand clothes and books, hippy jewellery, aromatherapy oils, candles and old Cat Stevens records.

Balmain Market

Milling around the shady grounds of St Andrew's Congregational Church, Balmain Market features stalls selling arts, crafts, books, clothing, jewellery, plants, and fruit and veg.

Paddington Markets

Sydney's best-attended weekend market coughs up everything from vintage clothes and hip fashion to jewellery, books, massage and palmistry. Parking is a misery – take public transport.

Rozelle Collectors Markets

One of Sydney's best bargain-hunter markets, with very few tourists. Sift through jewellery, clothes, plants, books and knick-knackery, with live folk music as a backdrop.

Paddington Markets

Cinema Under the Stars

Sunset Cinema

At picturesque North Sydney Oval, this outdoor cinema is one of several popular summer-night choices. Take snacks, but no booze: it's licensed.

Moonlight Cinema

Take a picnic and join the bats under the stars in magnificent Centennial Park; enter via the Woollahra Gate on Oxford St. A mix of new-release blockbuster, kid-friendly, art-house and classic films is screened at sunset from December to March.

OpenAir Cinema

Risk being distracted by the incredible city views where the screen juts up over the water at Mrs Macquarie's Point from early January to mid-February.

Bondi Openair Cinema

The slow, sexy grind of the surf adds to the mood from February to mid-March.

Inner West Openair Cinema

Students celebrate the end of exams at this pet-friendly location right on the harbour with a three-storey screen. Sunsets, skyline views, and swanky food and wine are on offer in December.

Ice Cream, Coffee & Cake

Bourke Street Bakery $

A Surry Hills institution, now spreading through Sydney to Marrickville and beyond.

Pablo & Rusty's Sydney CBD $

With the city centre's best coffee, this place means you don't even need to go to Melbourne.

Black Star Pastry $

Gourmet pies and delicious sweets, including its social-media star, watermelon cake, in colourful Newtown.

Koi Dessert Bar

Reuben Hills $$

The star is the fantastic single-origin coffee, roasted on the premises in Surry Hills, but the refreshing homemade horchata (rice milk), stellar fried chicken, tacos and *baleadas* (Honduran tortillas) are no slouches either.

Cow & the Moon $

This fabulous Enmore ice-creamery was crowned as purveyor of the world's best gelato in 2014 at the Gelato World Tour in Rimini, Italy.

Grounds of the City $$

You won't notice the crowds of the QVB inside this Parisian-style cafe. An oasis of vintage decor and excellent coffee, this is a recharging pit stop on any city-centre adventure.

Koi Dessert Bar $$$

MasterChef Australia star Reynold Poernomo produces his fabulous desserts by Central Park. Downstairs is a cafe with scrumptious sweet fare. Pre-book and head upstairs for the luxurious four-course dessert degustation.

Scan to find more things to do in Sydney online

07 Blue Mountains
MAGIC

VINTAGE | CULTURE | VIEWS

▬▬▬ A favourite rest stop for high society in the 1800s, the Blue Mountains region has luxury and style in spades. Explore arts, culture and architecture, eat lunch in a cosy cafe or drink an artisanal cocktail in an atmospheric bar. After you've recharged your batteries indoors, venture out into the area's glorious natural bounty.

INVISIBLESANE/SHUTTERSTOCK ©

⌖ How to

Getting here Trains on the Blue Mountains line leave regularly from Sydney's Central Station. The gateway town of Glenbrook is about an hour by car along the Great Western Hwy from Sydney.

When to go March and April, with light crowds, is a great time to hike. Avoid hot, busy December through February.

Call ahead Some shops and restaurants are closed on Monday, and local businesses close early on the weekend.

SLOW WALKER/SHUTTERSTOCK ©

SIDE TRIP BLUE MOUNTAINS MAGIC

Indoor Pursuits

Champagne Charlie's cocktail bar in Katoomba's historic Carrington Hotel (1883) transports you to a bygone era of glitz, glamour and free-flowing sparkling wine. Take a seat under the stained-glass dome and choose from a menu of traditional and modern cocktails, an extensive range of wines, and beer from the Carrington's own Katoomba Brewing Company.

Drawing its inspiration from Shanghai teahouses, the Hydro Majestic Hotel's **Salon du Thé** encompasses the building's former Billiards Room and Cats Alley ladies' lounge. Have an afternoon pot of tea after walking in the gardens, or try one of the unique, tea-inspired cocktails before dining at the hotel's **Wintergarden** restaurant.

WENDELL TEODORO/GETTY IMAGES ©

▣ Salacious Australian Art

The historic house of renowned Australian artist and author Norman Lindsay now showcases his numerous paintings, sculptures, etchings, and illustrations from his children's novel *The Magic Pudding*. Expect lush gardens, unique art and a view into Lindsay's sometimes scandalous life.

Left Hydro Majestic Hotel **Above left** Viewpoint overlooking the Three Sisters **Above right** Carrington Hotel

Vintage Shopping

Hunt for treasure in this popular antiquing destination. Run by veteran art and antiques dealer Steven Archer, the **Katoomba Antique Centre** also contains a small camera museum. Vinyl enthusiasts shouldn't miss the nearby **Velvet Fog Record Bar**, with a wide range of rare albums. **MacArthur's Arcade** has everything from china to furniture to vintage clothing. Downstairs is **Mr Pickwick's Books**, home to 60,000 vintage and secondhand volumes, and across the road in the old post office is the **Katoomba Vintage Emporium**.

Vintage-clothing enthusiasts will love **Leura Vintage**, with its wonderful array of fabulous frocks, and **Hazelbrook Cottage Antique Centre** offers a rustic collection of furniture and period Australiana.

🧍 Hiking the Blue Mountains

Prince Henry Cliff Walk
Connecting Katoomba and Leura, this moderate hike passes the famed Three Sisters, with views of Ruined Castle and three waterfalls. The track follows the base of the cliffs that make up Katoomba and Leura, allowing you to view the Jamison Valley from the ground floor.

Six Foot Track This beloved multiday hike (46km) follows a heritage horse trail and links Katoomba to the Jenolan Caves, allowing unfiltered views of the Megalong Valley.

For significant hikes, fill out a trip intention form, and borrow a personal locator beacon from a tourist-information centre or police station.

Left Grose Valley **Far left** Prince Henry Cliff Walk **Below** Red Hands Cave

Outdoor Delights

Hiking in Blackheath is almost synonymous with the Grand Canyon walk, but there are many easier and less-crowded walks that don't skimp on beautiful views of the Grose Valley. The **Fairfax heritage walk** is a level 1.8km track that is entirely wheelchair accessible. Visit in spring to see the waratahs and vibrant wildflowers in full bloom.

The whimsical name, relatively short distance and swimming hole at the end make the **Jellybean track** a favourite with outdoorsy families. Beyond the Jellybean Pool is the **Red Hands Cave**. View axe-carving grooves and the vibrant hand-stencil gallery created by the local Dharug people. The stencils in the Red Hands cave are between 500 and 1600 years old and are some of the best hand-stencil art in Sydney and its surrounds.

Pies & Sweet Treats

Every Australian town has a pie shop that you absolutely must try, and Blackheath is no different. The **Bakehouse on Wentworth** is a local and tourist favourite, with unforgettable pies. This is a great place to fuel up before heading off on a hike.

A staple in many children's trips to the Blue Mountains, the **Leura Lolly Shop** has walls lined with boiled lollies and chocolates ranging from Australian classics to modern and imported sweets.

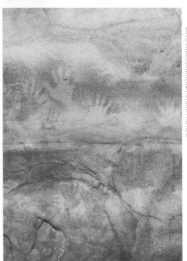

08 Fine Newcastle
FARE

CHIC CAFES | HIP BARS | EAT STREETS

▬▬ Once a gritty industrial city, today's Newcastle – affectionately known as 'Newy' – has transformed into one of Australia's most happening dining destinations. With an ever-increasing array of cool cafes, top-notch restaurants and buzzy bars, and the Hunter Valley wine region right on its doorstep, it's the kind of place where you'll want to arrive hungry – and thirsty.

ALEX JACK PHOTOGRAPHY ©

🗺 How to

Getting around Cruise between eateries on an e-bike for just $2 per 10 minutes or $10 per day courtesy of Newcastle's Bykko scheme.

When to go April is Newcastle Food Month, with oodles of culinary events, masterclasses, 'plate date' deals and more.

Stay Splash out on a night at Crystalbrook Kingsley, the city's first five-star hotel, where rooftop restaurant Roundhouse serves up city views with hearty Mod Oz fare that celebrates local and sustainable produce.

FORT WHISKEY PTY LTD ©

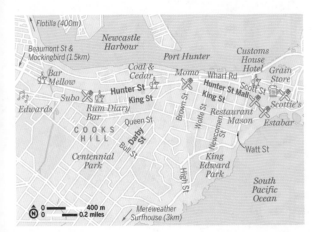

Far left top French toast, Momo **Far left bottom** Coal & Cedar

Cool Cafes

This relaxed seaside city was made for cafe culture. For ocean views with your smoked-salmon bagel, head to **Mereweather Surfhouse**, or tuck into scrambled eggs with macadamia pesto at **Estabar**, opposite Newcastle's main beach. In the city centre, **Momo** serves an innovative all-vegan menu (though cow's milk is available for coffees), while **Mockingbird** in Hamilton is the place to go when you're in the mood to pair your morning coffee with something more adventurous than avo toast – coconut satay French toast, perhaps?

Top Tables

Newcastle's fine-dining scene is on the up, with Australia's lauded *Good Food Guide* recently recognising **Restaurant Mason**, **Subo** and **Flotilla** for their innovative modern Australian menus, and **Scottie's** for its to-die(t)-for seafood dishes, including the moreish lobster, hash brown and sambal club sandwich.

Eat Streets

Newcastle has birthed several 'eat streets' packed with restaurants and bars. Among the best known is **Darby St** in Cooks Hill, just south of the city centre, where you'll find more than 20 restaurants, bars and cafes along a 400m stretch between Queen and Bull Sts. In Hamilton, west of the city centre, **Beaumont St** offers antique shopping by day and a thriving bar and restaurant scene by night. Right in the city, **King St** and **Hunter St** are also packed with drinking and dining options.

Bar Hopping

Edwards Co-founded by ex-Silverchair bassist Chris Joannou, this launderette conversion rocks from breakfast to happy hour, with regular live music.

Coal & Cedar Cocktails are mixed with flair at this hard-to-find New York–style speakeasy.

Rum Diary Bar This quirky bar's take on the classic dark-and-stormy is a crowd favourite.

Bar Mellow Sip minimal-intervention wines from the Hunter Valley and beyond.

Grain Store With a rotating selection of 21 craft beers on tap, this warehouse-turned-bar is a top spot for a pint and a burger.

Customs House Hotel Drink in the history of this watering hole, which has a great beer garden.

BYRON BAY & NORTH COAST NEW SOUTH WALES

BEAUTIFUL BEACHES | RAINFOREST HIKING | COASTAL DINING

Experience Byron Bay & North Coast NSW online

DARREN TIERNEY/SHUTTERSTOCK ©

BYRON BAY & NORTH COAST NSW
Trip Builder

Lush farmlands and pockets of World Heritage–listed rainforest fringe lazy beach towns all the way along the North Coast of New South Wales, many of them now just as well known for their culinary offerings as for their surf breaks and laid-back vibe.

Eat and drink your way around the **Tweed** (p80)
🚗 30mins from Byron Bay

BRISBANE

Surfers Paradise

Tweed Heads

Byron Bay

Rise early with the locals in **Byron Bay** (p82)
✈ 1½hrs from Sydney

Lismore

Casino

Ballina

QUEENSLAND

NEW SOUTH WALES

Moree

Yamba

Take a cultural stand-up paddleboarding (SUP) adventure on the **Coffs Coast** (p88)
🚗 2½hrs from Byron Bay

Grafton

South Pacific Ocean

Coffs Harbour

Hike behind a fairy-tale waterfall in **Dorrigo National Park** (p92)
🚗 1hr from Coffs Harbour

Nambucca Heads

South West Rocks

Tamworth

Kempsey

Port Macquarie

Scuba dive with endangered grey nurse sharks at **South West Rocks** (p94)
🚗 1¼hrs from Coffs Harbour

Taree

Forster-Tuncurry

Glamp with koalas in **Port Stephens** (p96)
🚗 2½hrs from Sydney

Port Stephens

Newcastle

NICK FOX/SHUTTERSTOCK ©

Explore bookable experiences in Byron Bay & North Coast NSW online

0 — 100 km
0 — 50 miles

Practicalities

ARRIVING

Gold Coast Airport Convenient entry point to the Tweed region.

Ballina Byron Gateway Airport Shuttles and taxis run to Byron Bay.

Coffs Harbour Airport Receives domestic flights from major cities.

CONNECT

Wi-fi is typically free at hotels but not always available at cafes; purchase a local SIM card to stay connected.

MONEY

You'll pay Sydney prices for food and lodgings in the Byron Bay region. Expect a 10–15% dining surcharge on Sundays.

WHERE TO STAY

Location	Atmosphere
Tweed Coast & Hinterland	Small boutique hotels and B&Bs.
Byron Bay	Boutique hotels, hostels, holiday apartments and campgrounds aplenty. Book ahead.
Mid-North Coast	Family-friendly resorts and campgrounds.
Barrington Coast	Ideal base for a budget family beach holiday.
Port Stephens	Smart boutique resorts, B&Bs and camping.

EATING & DRINKING

The northern end of the North Coast has an exciting culinary scene, with wholesome cafe fare and relaxed coastal fine dining showcasing local seafood and, increasingly, native ingredients. The trend is rapidly filtering southward, adding new options to towns along the coast.

Best coastal fine diner
Pipit, Pottsville (p81; pictured top)

Must-try craft beer
Stone & Wood Pacific Ale (p98; pictured bottom)

GETTING AROUND

Hire car & camper
Renting a car is the best way to explore. Bookings are required for camping in all NSW national parks; free camping is prohibited by some councils.

Taxi & ride share
Both widely available, but best booked ahead.

Train & bus A train service runs from Sydney to Casino. Greyhound buses run from Sydney to Byron Bay.

DEC–FEB
Ideal beach weather; book accommodation well ahead

MAR–MAY
Warm days with fewer crowds, except at busy Easter

JUN–AUG
Cooler temps perfect for hiking; still warm enough for a swim

SEP–NOV
Spring flowers, warm days and fewer crowds

09 Eat the **TWEED**

GOURMET PRODUCE | CRAFT DRINKS | COUNTRY DRIVES

At NSW's northeastern tip, the Tweed region's rich volcanic soils brim with fresh produce, which travels just metres to the plates of the region's ever-increasing array of restaurants. Home to one of the Tweed's top tables (Paper Daisy), the Hamptons-meets-NSW-coast Halcyon House hotel makes a fine base to explore the exciting local food and drinks scene between beach swims.

ARTUR BEGEL/SHUTTERSTOCK ©

🗺 How to

Getting around Navigating the Tweed's winding hinterland roads in a hire car is all part of the experience.

When to go Here you can top off a great meal with a swim in the sea year-round.

Burringbar This tiny hinterland village has a cheesemaker, an authentic Mexican takeaway and an artisan drinks tasting room.

Festival Indulge in a weekend of bespoke food experiences at November's Tweed Artisan Food Weekend.

EARTH BEER COMPANY ©

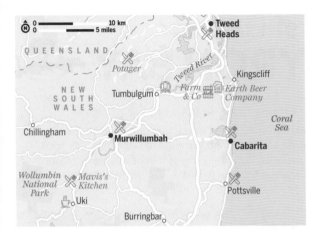

Top tables Multi-hatted chef Steve Snow put the Tweed on Australia's culinary map when he moved his Byron seafood restaurant, **Fins**, to Kingscliff in 2007. But it wasn't until **Paper Daisy** came along in 2015 with its creative Mod Oz dishes that the Tweed became a bona fide gourmet destination. In 2019 Paper Daisy chef Ben Devlin moved on to open **Pipit**, his own coastal fine diner in nearby Pottsville, to acclaim. 'Italian-ish' Cabarita restaurant **No.35 Kitchen and Bar** followed in 2021, along with Murwillumbah's **Tweed River House**, which also centres its creations on the seasonal harvest. Deeper in the hinterland, **Potager** and **Mavis's Kitchen** feature produce from their own kitchen gardens on their hearty lunch menus.

Drinks Coffee shops don't get much more atmospheric than **Bastion Lane Espresso**, set in a historic Uki post office. In Tumbulgum, **Husk Distillers** offers tours and tastings of its iconic Ink Gin and Agricole rums made with local sugar-cane juice. On an avocado farm in Cudgen, **Earth Beer Company** serves its eco-conscious craft brews in a lovingly restored packing shed.

Farm gates Shop for farm-fresh produce at **Farm & Co** or come for brunch overlooking the organic farm in Cudgen. Five minutes down the road, **Tropical Fruit World** has a stall brimming with everything from dragon fruit to mangoes. There's a cafe here too, and family-friendly tractor farm tours.

Far left top Fresh oysters **Far left bottom** Earth Beer Company brews

Did Someone Say Oysters?

In the Tweed you're never far away from fresh seafood, and at the **Oyster Shed** in Tweed Heads you can feast on oysters that have been farmed right in front of you.

Another fun way to sample local seafood is on a tour with **Catch a Crab**, run by the same company. Trap live crabs, go 'pumping' for yabbies and learn about the region's working oyster farms on a 2½-hour boat tour on the Tweed River. Spanner crabs, mud crabs and sand crabs are all found there at various times of the year.

10 First Light in **BYRON BAY**

SALUTE THE SUN | CULTURAL WALKS | COOL CAFES

Australia's most easterly town, Byron Bay is the first place on the mainland to see the dawn. Best viewed from the cliffs of Cape Byron, topped by a 1901 lighthouse, this soul-stirring experience is just one of many reasons to rise early with the locals, when this North Coast NSW holiday town is at its most serene.

📱 **How to**

When to go Late May to early November for whale watching, or the March–May and September–November shoulder seasons for warm beach weather with fewer crowds.

Wildlife Wallabies often graze on the cape in the early mornings.

Free yoga Hotels including Elements of Byron and Crystalbrook Byron offer complimentary morning yoga.

Surf lesson For one-on-one tuition, try Rusty Miller Surf, run by the local surfing identity and his daughter Taylor.

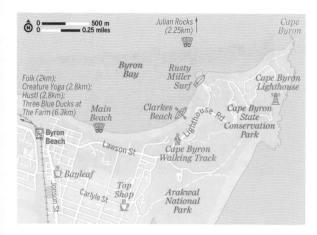

Far left top Sunrise, Main Beach
Far left bottom Surfer, Byron Bay

Seize the Morning

On land Many locals begin their day with an invigorating walk on the **Cape Byron Walking Track**, which makes a 3.7km loop around the rainforest-clad headland. If you begin early enough, you can enjoy the sunrise en route. Whales swim close to the cape, and dolphins can be spotted year-round, along with turtles, sharks and rays when the ocean is calm and clear.

The walking track also forms part of the **Byron Bay History Trail**; look out for the QR codes revealing insights into the early days of British settlement. To learn more about the deep cultural significance of Byron to Arakwal Bundjalung people, book a walking tour with Traditional Custodian Delta Kay of **Explore Byron Bay**.

In the water Beat the crowds by paddling out for a **surf** before sunrise, when you can also score a parking spot without too much effort. With the wind often picking up later in the day, aim for an early-morning **scuba dive** at Julian Rocks (Nguthungulli). There are two shipwrecks you can **snorkel** independently right off Main Beach; calm sea days are also ideal for an early-morning **kayaking tour** (two operators are based at Clarkes Beach).

At the studio Whether you're into yoga, pilates, barre or ice baths, Byron has your morning wellness routine covered. Local favourites include **Creature Yoga** for holistic classes, and **Hustl** for innovative and challenging cardio workouts.

 Brunch O'Clock

Bayleaf The Byron institution pairs smooth coffee with wholesome brunch dishes including the ever-popular scrambled special (eggs on sourdough with dill, chilli, marinated feta, salad greens and salsa verde).

Folk Near the northern entrance to town, this relaxed garden cafe presents its plant-based dishes beautifully.

Top Shop The former 1950s milk bar opens onto a grassy knoll, perfect for relaxing with a latte and an açai bowl or pastry.

Three Blue Ducks at The Farm Ideal for families: kids can meet the farm animals or hit the playground while parents linger over a decadent brunch showcasing homegrown produce.

The Byron Bay Experience

PARADISE REDEFINED

Between its eye-watering property prices and trending eateries, today's Byron Bay is a bit different from the sleepy coastal idyll 'discovered' by surfers in the 1950s, with hippies hot on their sandy heels. Scratch Byron's highly Instagrammable surface, however, and you'll discover a destination that still has plenty of substance.

Left Surfers, Byron Bay **Middle** Cape Byron Lighthouse **Right** Cafe, Byron Bay

'Cheer up, slow down, chill out', goes the welcome sign at the northern entrance to Byron Bay. The middle part of this mantra is easy enough to master, as you'll likely find yourself in a queue of traffic by the time you see it.

Such are the trade-offs of the ever-increasing popularity of this iconic Northern Rivers beach town, which now receives more than 2.2 million visitors per year – that's around 240 tourists for each of its 9200-odd residents. But dramatic headlines describing Byron as a 'paradise lost' only tell one side of the story.

An important meeting place for Bundjalung nation clans for more than 22,000 years, this genetically blessed corner of NSW – known as Gabanbaa to the local Arakwal people – changed forever when European settlers arrived in the late 1800s. First cedar-getters and farmers set about felling a 750-sq-km swathe of tropical lowland rainforest stretching from Byron to Lismore known as the Big Scrub; only 1% of this still stands today. Then sand-mining operations turned Byron's exquisite coastline into a barren wasteland. More extractive industries followed, with the Byron Bay township of the 1950s and '60s described in local historical records as 'reeking from the stench' of local piggery, meatworks and whaling factories.

It wasn't until these industries had all wound down by the early 1980s that Byron (originally named Cavvanba, an Anglicised version of Gabanbaa) began to transform back into a version of the paradise maintained by the Arakwal, who secured a historic Indigenous Land Use Agreement in 2001 that led to the formation of Arakwal National Park. Industrial workers transitioned to jobs in the service

industry, including tourism, and proposed developments with the potential to compromise the regeneration of Byron's natural environment, or the lifestyles of its new wave of alternative, eco-conscious locals, were passionately resisted.

Byron Today

That today's Byron is still a low-rise beach town in a gorgeous natural setting with a strong community spirit despite the increasing pressures of housing (un)affordability, climate change and urban development is really quite extraordinary. And while locals may complain about how busy, expensive

> This iconic Northern Rivers beach town now receives more than 2.2 million visitors per year.

and pretentious their home has become, many will concede that Byron's popularity has its benefits, the town now boasting one of Australia's finest regional dining scenes, a packed calendar of cultural events and a booming sustainable-fashion industry. Dotted with lauded restaurants and independent boutiques of their own, hinterland villages such as Bangalow and Federal, as well as nearby beach towns including Brunswick Heads and Lennox Head, have also become destinations in their own right.

Sure, reality-TV stars might now outnumber barefoot surfers at the Beach Hotel. And the days of scoring Byron's famous waves to yourself are long gone. But it's impossible to deny that Byron is still a special place.

🌱 How to 'Do' Byron

While it may seem more environmentally and socially responsible to stay away from destinations struggling with overtourism, planning an eco-conscious visit that supports the local community is often a more sustainable choice.

In Byron, this means avoiding unhosted holiday rentals outside the town centre, which are a major contributor to Byron's housing crisis; and supporting locally owned businesses committed to sustainable operations, so your money benefits the community as well as the environment. It means treading gently on the fragile ecosystem, and respecting local culture and laws. These small gestures protect Byron's natural beauty and individual character.

LOCAL PRODUCE
from the Source

01 Crab, Tweed Heads

Three crab species are harvested from the Tweed River; go on a crab-catching adventure with Tweed Eco Cruises.

02 Seafood, Yamba

Also known for its prawns, Yamba is a popular place to hook snapper, flathead (pictured), whiting and more – or purchase it fresh or cooked from Yamba's Fisho.

03 Macadamias, Byron Bay Hinterland

The birthplace of Australia's commercial macadamia-farming industry remains a great place to sample this rich, buttery native nut.

04 Bananas, Coffs Harbour

Did you even go on an East Coast road trip if you didn't get a selfie at the Big Banana?

05 Strawberries, Port Macquarie

Pick your own hydro-ponic strawberries year-round at Ricardoes, just off the Pacific Hwy north of the Hastings River.

06 Honey, Taree

Fragrant, gooey honey is a staple at Taree's

excellent Thursday Produce Market.

07 Oysters, Central Coast

Slurp down Sydney rock and Pacific oysters at the Hawkesbury River Oyster Shed, just off the highway at Mooney Mooney.

08 Prawns, Ballina

The home of the Big Prawn is famous for its local shellfish, known for their larger size and sweeter taste.

09 Avocados, Port Stephens

Pick up fresh, creamy avocados at the Bobs Farm Avocados stall on Nelson Bay Rd from June to November.

10 Artisan cheese, Macleay Valley Coast

This fertile farming region also produces delicious buffalo cheeses; try them at Eungai Creek Buffalo's cafe in Tamban.

11 Wine, Hunter Valley

Less than an hour inland from Newcastle, the Hunter Valley is Australia's oldest wine-growing region, with more than 150 cellar doors.

11 Coffs Coast
CULTURE

SACRED SITES | ADVENTURE | BUSH TUCKER

Known for its Big Banana and string of beautiful beaches, the Coffs Coast also has a rich Aboriginal culture. This is Gumbaynggirr Country, home to one of the largest coastal Aboriginal nations in NSW. Gumbaynggirr people have maintained a profound connection to the natural landscape, and this connection can be explored through experiences ranging from dance to a paddling tour.

WAJAANA YAAM ADVENTURE TOURS ©

🗺 **How to**

Cost A 2½-hour SUP tour with Wajaana Yaam Adventure Tours costs $169/71.50 for adults/ children eight and above. Younger kids paddle free.

Just passing through Nyanggan Gapi Cafe also operates a coffee van on Bray St, Coffs Harbour.

Solitary Islands Coastal Walk The 60km trail passes several cultural sites, including Look At Me Now Headland at Emerald Beach, which plays an integral part in the Creation story of Gumbaynggirr Country.

LYNNEBECLU/GETTY IMAGES ©

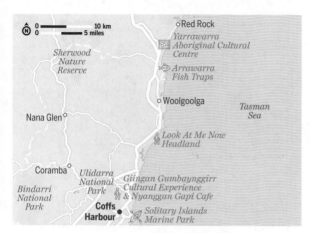

Far left top Stand-up paddleboarding with Wajaana Yaam Adventure Tours
Far left bottom Warrigal greens

Cultural paddle Hosted on three culturally significant creek systems in the Solitary Islands Marine Park, stand-up paddle-boarding excursions with **Wajaana Yaam Adventure Tours** pair fun on the water with fascinating insights into the Gumbaynggirr connection to this idyllic ecosystem. Along the way, your guide will share Dreaming stories, reveal the traditional uses of local plants and collect bush tucker to sample.

Aboriginal art & dance At Corindi Beach, the **Yarrawarra Aboriginal Cultural Centre** is home to the Wadjar Regional Indigenous Gallery and the Jalumbo Keeping Place. Here you can see paintings, ceramics, prints, photos and sculpture by regional Aboriginal artists, and view artefacts representing more than 4000 years of Aboriginal life in the area.

You can also learn about Gumbaynggirr culture through stories, song and dance during the **Giingan Gumbaynggirr Cultural Experience** led by the Bularri Muurlay Nyanggan Aboriginal Corporation. Watch the Wajaarr Ngaarlu dancers perform and take part in a smoking ceremony before enjoying Aunty Jenny's damper. Then you'll join an interpretative walk along the Gumgali Track to scenic Korora Lookout.

Indigenous food Try a 'roo burger with warrigal greens (native spinach) at the Yarrawarra Aboriginal Cultural Centre's **Pipeclay Cafe**, or head to the **Nyanggan Gapi Cafe** at Niigi Niigi (Sealy Lookout) to try Indigenous flavours in a wattleseed brownie or a lemon-myrtle muffin.

 Arrawarra Fish Traps

'On the northern side of the Arrawarra Headland, a series of stone fish traps appear at low tide. Dated to be around 5000 years old, the Arrawarra fish traps form an important part of a wider cultural landscape in Gumbaynggirr Country that Gumbaynggirr people have a continuing connection to. Highlighting the ingenuity of local Aboriginal people since time immemorial, the traps are a complex structure and the practices for using them are also complex, involving Gumbaynggirr language, song and an innate connection with ocean, dolphins and seasonal changes.'

 ■ **Clark Webb,** *Gumbaynggirr man, CEO of the Bularri Muurlay Nyanggan Aboriginal Corporation and owner-operator of Wajaana Yaam Adventure Tours* @wajaanayaam

12 Gondwana Hikes
GALORE

RAINFOREST | HIKING | WATERFALLS

Comprising more than 30 national parks and reserves between southeast Queensland and Newcastle, the Unesco-listed Gondwana Rainforests of Australia holds the world's most extensive areas of subtropical rainforest. Get your Gondwana fix on these great hikes near the coast in the NSW section.

How to

Getting around You'll need your own car to access most Gondwana parks.

When to go Hiking is excellent year-round, though the risk of dehydration and heat stroke increases in summer.

Safety Always tell someone where you're going and when you plan to return, and pack adequate water and gear.

Parks pass Visiting several NSW national parks with parking fees? It may be cheaper to purchase an annual multi-parks pass ($45; nationalparks.nsw. gov.au).

Minyon Falls Loop, Nightcap National Park

Distance 13km

Duration Three to four hours

Just 45 minutes west of Byron Bay, this hike takes you from the top of Minyon Falls to the base of the magnificent waterfall, some 100m below. Tracing the Nightcap escarpment, the track begins in wet sclerophyll forest before descending into a cooler subtropical wonderland as the rainforest canopy closes in towards the bottom of the valley. Enjoy a dip in the natural waterfall pool before hiking up the other side of the escarpment for front-on views of the falls from the Minyon Grass Picnic Area before walking back to the trailhead along the road (1km).

(i) Bushfires

More than 50% of the Gondwana Rainforests burned during Australia's 2019–20 bushfires, and the habitats of rare and threatened flora and fauna suffered catastrophic damage. Nearly all affected tourism infrastructure has since reopened, though, and the rainforest continues to recover with the assistance of governments, Aboriginal groups, scientists and local communities.

Left Nightcap National Park **Above left** Minyon Falls **Above right** Kookaburra, Nightcap National Park

Iluka Rainforest Walking Track, Iluka Nature Reserve

Distance 5.2km return

Duration One to three hours

In Iluka Nature Reserve, near Yamba, the Iluka Rainforest Walking Track offers an easy stroll through lush coastal forest to Iluka Bluff in neighbouring Bundjalung National Park. Look out for the brightly coloured noisy pitta, and listen for the sharp crack of the whipbird. The Bluff is a great spot for a picnic lunch and a swim (or snorkel) before heading back the same way, with great whale watching from late May to early November.

Crystal Shower Walk, Dorrigo National Park

Distance 4.4km return

Duration 90 minutes

Mist-shrouded rainforest towers above you on this short but stunning walk in Dorrigo National Park, an hour's drive west of Coffs

🐦 Quirky Gondwana Wildlife

Alberts lyrebird Look for this shy bird scratching for soil-dwelling invertebrates. In winter and early spring you might hear the male's unique call mimicking sounds he's heard over the years, or see him do his magnificent tail fan dance.

Red-legged pademelon If you're still and quiet, you can see these small macropods feeding on fruit and leaves in the early morning and late afternoon.

Land mullet The largest member of the skink family is often mistaken for a snake.

Lamington crayfish Usually a bright turquoise, this large freshwater crayfish is typically seen in rainforest creeks above 300m.

■ **Wendy Bithell,**
ecotour guide and founder of Vision Walks Eco-Tours
@visionwalks

CHARLIE BLACKER/SHUTTERSTOCK ©

HAL BERAL/GETTY IMAGES ©

Left New England National Park **Far left** Red-legged pademelon **Below** Lamington crayfish

Harbour via the Waterfall Way scenic drive. The trail takes you behind the fairy-tale Crystal Shower Falls, and a suspension bridge carries you across the valley in front of the falls for Insta-worthy views. Return the same way or extend the walk by looping back via Tristania Falls on the Wonga Walk, which adds 2.2km to the journey. Don't miss the Skywalk Lookout next to the Rainforest Centre on your way out, nor the charming hinterland town of Bellingen on the drive back to the coast.

ANDYWAK/SHUTTERSTOCK ©

Eagles Nest Walking Track, New England National Park

Distance 2.2km loop

Duration One hour

An hour southwest of Dorrigo National Park, Point Lookout is one of NSW's most photographed sunrise spots. Several trails begin here, 1500m above sea level at the edge of the Great Escarpment. A highlight is the Eagles Nest Walking Track, which takes you past huge mossy Antarctic beech trees dotted with beech orchids. In winter, water trickling from the rocks often forms chandeliers of ice. While there are a few small climbs, this is an easily manageable trail for most walkers.

13

Dive into the
NORTH COAST

SHARK DIVING | SNORKELLING | MARINE WONDERS

The Great Barrier Reef isn't the only great place to go scuba diving in Australia. North Coast NSW is one of the best places in the world to dive with critically endangered grey nurse sharks, a large, placid species that gathers in several spots along the coast at different periods throughout the year.

ASHTONEX/SHUTTERSTOCK ©

🗺 How to

When to go The water temperature can dip below 20°C on the North Coast in winter, but there's no bad time of year to go diving (just bad weather). All operators rent wetsuits.

Qualification Some shark dive spots are suitable for open-water divers, while others require advanced open-water certification. Check with your operator.

Snorkelling There's great snorkelling at many dive sites; some operators allow snorkellers to join trips at a reduced cost.

ORION MEDIA GROUP/SHUTTERSTOCK ©

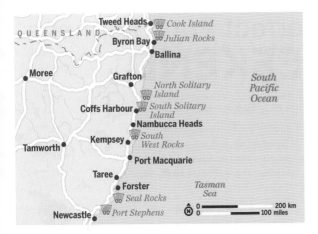

Far left top Grey nurse shark **Far left bottom** Green sea turtle, Julian Rocks

Shark Diving

Julian Rocks (Nguthungulli) Temperate and tropical waters meet at the rocky outcrop off Byron Bay known as Julian Rocks (Nguthungulli in the Bundjalung language), attracting marine life as abundant as it is diverse. Grey nurse sharks (which grow up to 3.6m long) congregate here from June to November, but as soon as they leave another major attraction arrives: beautifully patterned (and similarly docile) leopard sharks, which stick around until May, along with huge manta rays. Bottom-dwelling wobbegong sharks can be seen year-round.

South West Rocks Running 125m right through Fish Rock, which lies 2km off South West Rocks on the Mid-North Coast, Fish Rock Cave offers year-round grey nurse sightings, along with a plethora of other marine life, from moray eels to friendly blue groupers. In the summer months, grey nurse sharks rest in the azure cave entrance, presenting an incredible photographic opportunity. While Nitrox certification isn't essential, it's recommended for this dive.

Forster & Seal Rocks On the Barrington Coast, Forster and nearby Seal Rocks are home to more than a dozen dive sites. Many of these are also visited by grey nurse sharks year-round. Top picks include the Pinnacle, a deeper dive off Forster (where the dive operators are located), and Big Rock at Seal Rocks, which is surrounded by several gutters patrolled by graceful grey nurse sharks.

Other Fantastic North Coast Dives

Cook Island Green turtles are the main attraction at this relatively shallow dive site just off Tweed Heads.

North Solitary Island There are so many anemones in this section of the Solitary Islands Marine Park that the sea floor looks like a shag-pile carpet.

South Solitary Island This shallow dive site off Coffs Harbour is great for learning, and there's plenty of temperate marine life, similar to that of Byron Bay.

Port Stephens A popular dive site off Port Stephens is The Looking Glass at Broughton Island, a narrow trench where grey nurse sharks congregate.

■ Recommended by Georgie Loo, *scuba-diving instructor-trainer at Byron Bay Dive Centre* @byronbaydivecentre

14 A Perfect Port Stephens
WEEKEND

GREAT BEACHES | SCENIC WALKS | ICONIC WILDLIFE

Just two hours north of Sydney, Port Stephens offers the ultimate nature hit with its beaches, coastal walks, wildlife encounters and massive sand dunes surrounding an immense natural harbour. It always feels like the weekend here, where seafood rules local menus.

PETER K LEUNG/GETTY IMAGES ©

🗺 Trip Notes

Getting around There's a good local bus network, including services to Newcastle.

When to go October to April for wild dolphin swims; mid-May to early November for whale watching.

Seafood Try Little Nel, Little Beach Boathouse, Rick Stein at Bannisters, and Sandpiper, or grab a tray of fresh oysters at Holberts Oyster Farm.

Local tipples Murray's Craft Brewing Co shares its home with Port Stephens Winery; sample both at its HQ overlooking a vineyard.

🐋 Dolphins & Whales

Port Stephens is famous for its bottlenose dolphins. Humpback whales (pictured) join the party in winter, making it a great time to book a cetacean-watching cruise. You can also opt to 'join the pod' with Dolphin Swim Australia, which holds a permit from NSW Parks to operate responsible wild dolphin swims.

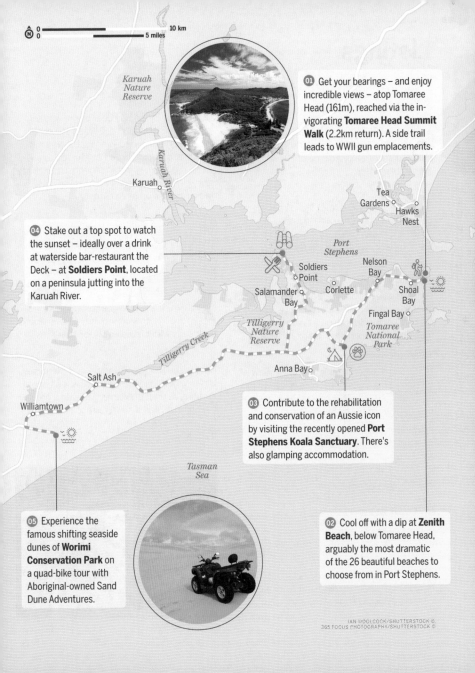

0 km / 0 — 10 km
0 / 0 — 5 miles
Ⓝ

Karuah Nature Reserve

Karuah River

Karuah

01 Get your bearings – and enjoy incredible views – atop Tomaree Head (161m), reached via the invigorating **Tomaree Head Summit Walk** (2.2km return). A side trail leads to WWII gun emplacements.

Tea Gardens

Hawks Nest

Port Stephens

Nelson Bay

04 Stake out a top spot to watch the sunset – ideally over a drink at waterside bar-restaurant the Deck – at **Soldiers Point**, located on a peninsula jutting into the Karuah River.

Soldiers Point

Salamander Bay

Corlette

Shoal Bay

Fingal Bay

Tilligerry Nature Reserve

Tilligerry Creek

Tomaree National Park

Salt Ash

Anna Bay

Williamtown

03 Contribute to the rehabilitation and conservation of an Aussie icon by visiting the recently opened **Port Stephens Koala Sanctuary**. There's also glamping accommodation.

Tasman Sea

05 Experience the famous shifting seaside dunes of **Worimi Conservation Park** on a quad-bike tour with Aboriginal-owned Sand Dune Adventures.

02 Cool off with a dip at **Zenith Beach**, below Tomaree Head, arguably the most dramatic of the 26 beautiful beaches to choose from in Port Stephens.

Listings

BEST OF THE REST

Bakeries & Cafes

Cubby Bakehouse $

Opposite the Tweed River at Chinderah, this bakery-cafe has earned a cult following for its French baguettes.

Bruns Bakery $

This huge, busy Brunswick Heads bakery does a roaring trade in pies, pastries, bread, cakes and more. Has a similarly excellent sister bakery in Suffolk Park, Byron Bay.

Supply Coffee $

The micro-roastery, espresso bar and licensed cafe in Coffs Harbour's jetty precinct is a top spot for coffee, breakfast (from 6.30am) or lunch, with creative menu options including a blue-spanner-crab omelette.

Hilltop Store $$

Housed in a restored general store in Sawtell, this charming Coffs Coast cafe is known for its simple but refined breakfast and lunch menus, with coffee by Single O.

Fredo Pies $

In the small village of Frederickton, just off the Pacific Hwy north of Kempsey, this pie shop is an institution for East Coast road-trippers. The 25-plus options include a crocodile pie.

Craft Breweries

Seven Mile Brewing Co $

Next to Ballina's airport, family-run Seven Mile supports local grain growers to produce highly quaffable craft brews, including the refreshing Cali Cream ale. Food-truck fare is typically available Friday to Sunday.

Stone & Wood $

The famous Byron Bay beer brand was sold to Asahi in 2021, but Stone & Wood still serves the same multi-award-winning brews in its architect-designed brew bar. Guided tours reveal the brewery's pioneering sustainability story, and local catering company 100 Mile Table runs the on-site canteen.

Sanctus Brewing Company $$

There's plenty of indoor and outdoor seating at this large brewery, just off the Pacific Hwy near Yamba, with wood-fired pizzas also on the menu.

Woolgoolga Brewing Co $$

Opened in sleepy Woolgoolga (Woopi to locals) in 2021, this community brewery pairs craft suds with pizzas and good times.

Bucket Brewery $

Next to the Macleay River in South Kempsey, this family-owned brewery is about as unpretentious as craft breweries get, with a great beer garden, and a new live-music stage on the way. Check its Facebook page for food-truck info.

Seven Mile Brewing Co

King Tide Brewing $$

Also new in 2021, this 250-seat suburban beer oasis in central Coffs Harbour serves up a huge range of craft brews along with European-inspired pub grub, in a nod to co-owner Lucyna King's Polish heritage.

Bellingen Brewing Co. $$

This artisan brewery is an excellent reason to detour to the charming hinterland village of Bellingen, inland from Urunga on the Mid-North Coast. Also serves pizzas.

Regional Art Galleries

Tweed Regional Gallery & Margaret Olley Art Centre

The key draw of this lauded gallery, perched above the Tweed River, is the recreated studio of the late Margaret Olley, Australia's celebrated painter of still lifes and interiors.

Lismore Regional Gallery

Inland from Byron Bay, Lismore has a flourishing arts scene. After touring its modern gallery, where the permanent collection includes a fabulous series of photographs showcasing the 1973 Nimbin Aquarius Festival, seek out the vibrant street-art gallery nearby.

Coffs Regional Gallery

A highlight is the Robert & Janice Hunter Collection, donated to the gallery in 2018, featuring the works of 33 Aboriginal artists from Central Australia, the Kimberley and Arnhem Land.

Glasshouse Regional Gallery

The striking Port Macquarie arts hub show-cases up to 25 exhibitions per year featuring contemporary, Indigenous, historical, traditional, design and sculptural artworks, along with artist talks and workshops.

VISUAL COLLECTIVE/SHUTTERSTOCK ©

Surfer, Duranbah

Surf Spots Beyond Byron

Duranbah (D-bah)

Neighbouring Coolangatta's Snapper Rocks is one of the world's most famous surfing beaches. But just around the headland, NSW's north-ernmost beach produces consistent A-frame beach breaks. For more beginner-friendly waves, try Cabarita, 25 minutes south.

Angourie

NSW's first dedicated National Surfing Reserve, this Clarence Valley beach has an excellent right-hand point break, and natural freshwater swimming holes on the headland.

Arrawarra

On the northern fringe of the Coffs Coast, Arrawarra has an exposed right-hand point break with pretty consistent surf, ideal in off-shore winds from the southwest.

Crescent Head

Also a National Surfing Reserve, the right-hand point break at Crescent Head on the Macleay Valley Coast – which has a popular beachside holiday park – is legendary.

Scan to find more things to do in Byron Bay & North Coast NSW online

SOUTH COAST NEW SOUTH WALES

COASTAL | DELICIOUS | DIVERSE

Experience
South Coast
NSW online

GREG BRAVE/SHUTTERSTOCK ©

SOUTH COAST NSW
Trip Builder

Stretching to the very end of New South Wales, the South Coast is full of beautiful, quiet coastal towns. Far from just a haunt for suntanned surfers, the area is full of artisanal foods, natural wonders, and locals passionate about what makes their town uniquely theirs.

Find inner peace at the **Nan Tien Temple** (p107)
🚌 30mins from Wollongong CBD

Meet massive fish at the **Mollymook Bogey Hole** (p111)
🚶 15mins from Mollymook

Surf like a real Aussie at **Broulee South Beach** (p111)
🚗 10mins from Moruya

Taste Tilba heritage at the **ABC Cheese Factory** (p113)
🚶 10mins from Central Tilba

Blue Mountains National Park

● Goulburn

Morton National Park

A C T ✪ CANBERRA

Ulladulla

Batemans Bay

○ Mogo

Deua National Park

Moruya

○ Bodalla

Narooma ○

Wadbilliga National Park

○ Central Tilba
○ Bermagui

Bega

○ Tathra

○ Merimbula

○ Eden

Kosciuszko National Park

VICTORIA

N E W
S O U T H
W A L E S

○ Mallacoota

ABC CHEESE FACTORY

● Sydney

N 0 ———————————— 100 km
  0 ———————————— 50 miles

Royal
National
Park

● Wollongong

○ Port Kembla

○ Kiama

○ Berry

● Nowra

Cool down
after hiking to
**Wattamolla
Beach** (p109)
🚶 *2hrs from
Bundeena*

Explore the marshes by
paddleboard at **Lake
Conjola** (p111)
🚗 *15mins from Milton*

*South
Pacific
Ocean*

Gorge on gorgeous oysters
from the **Clyde River** (p113)
🚗 *1hr from Milton*

Swim with penguins and seals
at **Montague Island** (p111)
⛴ *20mins from Narooma*

*Tasman
Sea*

Uncover the mystery of the
SS *Ly-ee-Moon* at **Green
Cape Lighthouse** (p115)
🚗 *1hr from Eden*

**Explore bookable
experiences in
South Coast
NSW online**

Practicalities

ARRIVING

Illawarra/South Coast Line Intercity trains run from Sydney to Port Kembla, Kiama and Bomaderry.

Eden Premier Motor Services Offers a daily bus service from Sydney.

Merimbula Airport and Moruya Airport Rex and Qantas fly to both airports from Sydney.

HOW MUCH FOR A

250mL tube of sunscreen $7

Local cheese $12

Dozen oysters $20

GETTING AROUND

Car The South Coast is well connected by road. Between Tilba Tilba and Pambula, stick to the spectacular coastline on Bermagui Rd and the Sapphire Coast drive. Some areas lose internet reception, so have a map downloaded or a paper map on hand.

Bike Road biking between towns is a popular choice, but Berry and its surrounds are quite hilly.

Walking Historic towns like Milton and Central Tilba are best explored on foot.

WHEN TO GO

DEC–FEB
Hot and dry; school holidays in January

MAR–MAY
Wet becoming cool; fewer tourists after Easter

JUN–AUG
Frosty; whale-watching season; good surfing

SEP–NOV
Cool but gradually becoming warm and wet

EATING & DRINKING

The South Coast is known for its clean, sweet-tasting oysters. Pacific oysters are best from April to September, Angasi oysters are available from June to August, and Sydney rock oysters (pictured) are in season from November to March. Wines from the burgeoning Shoalhaven region profit from rich volcanic soil, and viticulturists have introduced several uncommon varietals. In the Eurobodalla region, try fresh-from-the-farm milks and cheeses.

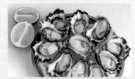

Best winery
Crooked River
Wines (p119)

Must-try oysters
Jim Wild's
Oysters (p113)

CONNECT & FIND YOUR WAY

Wi-fi South of the Illawarra, some towns have poor internet connection. Milton/Ulladulla are relatively well connected, but expect to unplug beyond the town centres in Eurobodalla Shire.

Navigation Like much of Australia, the South Coast can be deceptively large. It consists of several regions: the Illawarra, Shoalhaven, the Eurobodalla Shire and the Sapphire Coast. By car from Sydney, take the Princes Hwy/A1 south.

WHERE TO STAY

Accommodation is plentiful on the South Coast. Vacation rentals are a great option for larger groups. Book at least a month ahead in peak seasons, when prices often inflate.

Location	Atmosphere
Illawarra	Lively, youthful atmosphere. Plentiful accommodation. Towns are larger and harder to travel by foot.
Shoalhaven	Many beachfront hotels. Holiday parks and motor inns are common, with some holiday rentals. Family atmosphere. Fills up quickly in the summer months; can be quite expensive.
Eurobodalla	Quiet, countryside area. Smaller, boutique accommodation options. Great location for a farmstay.
Sapphire Coast	Beachfront locale. Holiday parks and motor inns are common. Often more affordable than Milton/Ulladulla.

PRIVATE LESSONS

Even inexperienced athletes can enjoy the beaches, with a private surf lesson averaging about $90. For the more adventurous, intro-ductory scuba courses cost about $150 per day.

MONEY

There are plenty of free outdoor activities in the area, from bushwalking to rock pooling to a day at the beach. Food – particularly oysters – is much cheaper on the South Coast than in Sydney, so you're likely to strike a bargain.

Sample a Millennial
SEA CHANGE

ENERGY | NIGHTLIFE | NATURE

Once supported by the steel and shipping industries, the Illawarra is growing in popularity among young people escaping the madness of living in Sydney. For Wollongong, affectionately shortened to just the 'Gong', the primary industry is the local university, lending the city and its surrounds a youthful energy.

TOM JEERASAK JINAKAN/SHUTTERSTOCK ©

How to

Getting here & around Much of the Illawarra is serviced by the South Coast train line from Sydney. Buses run on the Opal system, and the Free Gong Shuttle runs a regular circuit in Wollongong.

When to go Beachgoers will prefer the warmer months, and cocktail connoisseurs should avoid university orientation week in late February.

Aussie music Wollongong's beloved Yours and Owls music festival takes place on the first weekend of April.

NICK FOX/SHUTTERSTOCK ©

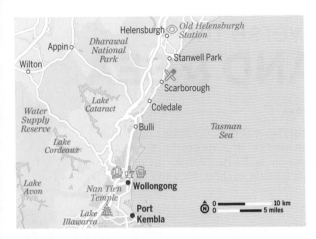

Far left top Nan Tien Temple **Far left bottom** Old Helensburgh Station

Glow-worm central The **Old Helensburgh Station** first began operating in the 1880s and was decommissioned in the 1920s. Now the former railway tunnel is home to a bright community of glow-worms. Their enchanting blue-green lights cover the roof and walls of the tunnel, and they're especially active during rainy periods. Glow-worms are sensitive to vibrations and external light, so keep your torch off for the best view. The ground can be wet and occasionally slippery, so do take care.

The Gong at night Spirit aficionados will find their home in **Howlin' Wolf** whisky bar, or the gin-focused **Births and Deaths**, housed in the former office of Births, Deaths and Marriages. The **Daring Squire** offers a more traditional pub feel, drawing its inspiration from Australia's first brewer, James Squire. For lunchtime fare, you can't pass up the **Scarborough Hotel**, with an expansive beer garden and cliffside views over the Pacific.

Tranquil Buddhist retreat The **Nan Tien Temple** (Southern Heaven Temple) is the largest Buddhist temple in the southern hemisphere. A testament to Australia's multiculturalism, the palatial temple was designed by Australian architects. Take advantage of the regular meditation classes and retreats, or take a peaceful walk through the gardens. Locals frequent the dining hall and teahouse. Both venues are famed for their entirely vegetarian menus.

⟨⟨⟨ Spectacular ≋ Blowholes

The sea makes an impressive entrance at the **Kiama Blowhole**, known as Khanterinte by the local Dharawal people. The show is caused by waves pushing water out of a pocket in the volcanic rock that makes up the shoreline. The best time to visit is when the wind is blowing southeast. Between May and November, the nearby picnic areas make a perfect whale-watching spot. Alternatively, head down to the **Blowhole Point Pools** for a safe ocean swim. Just 4km south is the **Little Blowhole**, which has more consistent displays that are best when the wind blows northeast.

16

Traverse the
LAND & SEA

VIEWS | WALKING | OUTDOORS

Situated within Royal National Park, the 26km Coast Track stretches between Bundeena and Otford. Cross clifftops, explore coastal heathland and take a dip in the Pacific. Hike the whole track over two days, or visit the sites as short day walks.

TRAVELLING ABOUT/ SHUTTERSTOCK ©

🌿 Track Ecology & Views

The track moves through rocky clifftops, beach, and coastal heathland. In springtime, experience the salty sea air give way to honeyed blossoms from the abundant native flora. Even after fire season, the lower levels of bushland regenerate quickly, demonstrating the perseverance of the Australian landscape. With heights of more than 1300m above sea level, the views to the sea are awe-inspiring.

🗺 Trip Notes

Stay hydrated Be sure to carry sufficient water or water-treatment options, as there is no access to drinking water on the walk.

Check the weather Some sections are steep and exposed, so it is not advised to hike during heavy rain or high winds.

Bring proper gear Waterproof shoes are a must, as you will be walking across creeks and beaches.

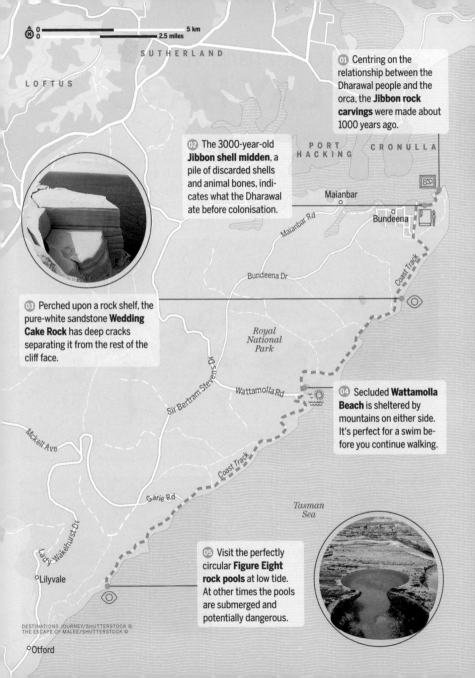

0 | 5 km
N
0 | 2.5 miles

SUTHERLAND

LOFTUS

01 Centring on the relationship between the Dharawal people and the orca, the **Jibbon rock carvings** were made about 1000 years ago.

02 The 3000-year-old **Jibbon shell midden**, a pile of discarded shells and animal bones, indicates what the Dharawal ate before colonisation.

PORT HACKING   CRONULLA

Maianbar

Bundeena

Maianbar Rd

Bundeena Dr

Coast Track

03 Perched upon a rock shelf, the pure-white sandstone **Wedding Cake Rock** has deep cracks separating it from the rest of the cliff face.

Royal National Park

Sir Bertram Stevens Dr

Wattamolla Rd

04 Secluded **Wattamolla Beach** is sheltered by mountains on either side. It's perfect for a swim before you continue walking.

Mckell Ave

Coast Track

Garie Rd

Lady Wakehurst Dr

Lilyvale

Tasman Sea

05 Visit the perfectly circular **Figure Eight rock pools** at low tide. At other times the pools are submerged and potentially dangerous.

DESTINATIONS JOURNEY/SHUTTERSTOCK ©.
THE ESCAPE OF MALEE/SHUTTERSTOCK ©

Otford

Work Hard to
PLAY HARD

ECOLOGY | WATER SPORTS | OUTDOORS

If the sea breeze isn't enough to get your blood pumping, plenty of experiences in Shoalhaven and the Eurobodalla Shire will help that along. Activities like snorkelling, paddleboarding and hiking provide up-close encounters with the area's natural wonders, proving that 'relaxing' doesn't have to mean 'recumbent'.

PAPUDHALKA_KAELAIMAGES/SHUTTERSTOCK ©

📷 **How to**

Getting around Your own car is best for getting around, but most towns are connected by daily private charter bus.

When to go Die-hard surfers will prefer the waves in winter. The warmer months bring tourists, and the beaches can get crowded. Check the tides if you're planning to visit a beach, as different water levels are suited to different activities.

Montague Island Only NSW Parks and Wildlife Authority–approved vessels can access the island.

HORIZON INTERNATIONAL IMAGES LIMITED/ ALAMY STOCK PHOTO ©

Far left top Lake Conjola sand dunes
Far left bottom Diver and weedy sea dragon, Jervis Bay

Cycling Berry is a favourite with experienced cyclists for its steep descents and established cycling community. Hill-chasers will love the Block Rd ride, or reward yourself with a glass after riding to Two Figs Winery. You can also ride between towns, such as Ulladulla to Milton or Nowra to Huskisson. Mountain bikers should tackle the exhilarating Deep Creek Dam Loop in Mogo for views of Mogo State Forest.

SUP & fishing Stand-up paddleboarding is a unique way to tour the Narrawallee inlet and Lake Conjola. Many surf schools offer classes and rentals. The inlet is also a great fishing spot: expect to catch plenty of bream, whiting and flathead.

Diving & snorkelling In Mollymook the outer rock shelf of the Bogey Hole is a popular snorkelling location, home to some startlingly large blue gropers. Spot wobbegong sharks and manta rays atop Jervis Bay's famous white sand at Little Hymans Beach and Chinamans Beach. Experienced divers can explore the SS *Merimbula*, wrecked off the coast of Currarong and now considered a heritage wreck site. Near Eden, at Twofold Bay, the *Tasman Hauler* and *Henry Bolte* are two upright wrecks scuttled in the 1980s for diving purposes.

Surfing Beginners will appreciate Seven Mile Beach and Mollymook Beach, and Broulee South's variable swells will suit many different surfers at different times of the day.

Snorkel with the Seals

Secluded Montague Island lies off the Narooma coast. Attend a day tour or stay in one of the 1880s lighthouse-keeper's cottages. The local Yuin people know the island as Baranguba, and it was an important place for gathering food and conducting men's business.

The island is the breeding ground for NSW's largest little-penguin colony, and many other seabirds nest here over summer. Fur seals are plentiful in winter and spring, and in the crystal-clear waters, snorkellers and divers can see the seals at their most playful. Between September and November, Montague is a great place to spot humpback whales during their migration.

18 The Trail to Great CUISINE

FOOD | WINE | FRESH PRODUCE

Let your stomach lead the way as you explore the fresh, complex and invigorating flavours of the South Coast in Shoalhaven and the Eurobodalla Shire. Taste the difference in your seafood when it's fresh from the sea, and experience the freshness of farm-to-table eating. Here you can find new favourites or try variations on old ones.

How to

Getting around Your own car is best for getting around, but most towns are connected by daily private charter bus.

When to go Foods are generally available year-round. Many cafes and restaurants are closed Monday to Wednesday, especially in low season.

Love your oysters If you're planning to follow the oyster trail, bring an Esky. This Aussie icon will help keep your purchases cool (but it won't stop you eating them all on the spot).

Map:
Goulburn — Kiama — Berry — Gerringong — Silos Estate — Nowra — Two Figs — Morton National Park — Cupitt's Estate — Ulladulla — Batemans Bay — Mogo — Deua National Park — Bodalla — Narooma — Tasman Sea — ABC Cheese Factory — Bermagui
50 km / 25 miles

Slow food Many places emphasise permaculture, organic gardening and farm-to-table eating. Taste the region's best produce at weekly farmers markets in Kiama and Berry. Charming, family-run **Buena Vista** farm in Gerringong offers classes in cooking, fermentation and organic gardening.

Top-notch dairy Milk with the cream still at the top. Ice cream churned by hand. Butter you can see the salt flakes in. Sample all this and more at South Coast dairies. **Narooma Ice Creamery**, with a diversity of flavours, is a favourite with families. Micro-dairy the **Bodalla Dairy Shed** bottles all its milk in-house.

Right top Two Figs wine with picnic spread **Right bottom** Bottle-fed calf, Bodalla Dairy Shed

🚚 Year-Round Oysters

Oysters are the essential South Coast seafood, with three varieties farmed locally: Sydney rock, Angasi and Pacific. Try them from the farm at **Jim Wild's**, open since 1979, or the **Bateman's Bay Oyster Shed**, with a side of Clyde River views. Other great purveyors include the **Oyster Farmer's Daughter** and the **Narooma Quarterdeck**.

Try it in milkshakes and ice creams, or sample its cheeses, many of which are flavoured with native bush tucker. For a taste of history, visit the 1891 **ABC Cheese Factory**, now home to the award-winning cheeses of **Tilba Real Dairy**.

Uncommon wines Though not as well known as other NSW wine regions, the Shoalhaven Coast has been producing great wines for 40 years. Viticulturists have taken advantage of the unique seaside terroir to explore uncommon varietals, particularly the grape of the Shoalhaven, chambourcin. **Cupitt's Estate** has a winery, craft brewery, fromagerie and restaurant. **Silos Estate** operates out of the buildings of an 1870s dairy farm, and also houses a working alpaca farm. For a more intimate experience, stop at **Two Figs**, which sources all its grapes from within the South Coast.

19

Travel Back
IN TIME

HISTORY | SCENERY | PROSPECTING

■■■■ Explore some of Australia's early colonial settlements, enjoying late Victorian and Federation-era architecture. Discover histories of gold fever and legacies of the region's enduring industries, such as 1890s dairy sheds that are still in use today. On the South Coast, you don't just learn about those who came before; you walk in their footsteps.

WIRESTOCK CREATORS/SHUTTERSTOCK ©

🗺 How to

Getting around Your own car is best for getting around, but most towns are connected by daily private charter bus.

When to go Avoid travelling from July to August if you're planning to hike, as the wind chill can be biting. In summer, seasonal bushfires may obstruct access to some of these locations.

Local historians Towns such as Milton have vibrant local-history societies that are happy to share their knowledge.

ALIZADA STUDIOS/SHUTTERSTOCK ©

Far left top Shopfront, Central Tilba
Far left bottom Eden Killer Whale Museum

Historic towns The colonial history of the South Coast dates to the late 1800s, and there are many picturesque towns if you fancy a trip back to last century.

Milton was established in the 1880s, and many of its original buildings are still in use. The main street is dotted with late-Victorian posted verandahs and corrugated roofs, and the 1930s Milton Theatre still houses live music and stage productions. Drive around the country roads to spot some of the original homesteads. Heritage-listed **Central Tilba** is a prime example of early colonial architecture. Originally a gold-mining town, Tilba was kept afloat by the dairy industry. This history continues at the ABC Cheese Factory, still operating from original 1890s dairy sheds. At nearby **Tilba Tilba**, you can pay your respects to the town's founders, interred at the district cemetery.

Gold fever In **Bermagui** a short-lived gold rush began in 1880 after the discovery of alluvial gold. This history can be explored at the Montreal Goldfield, the only goldfield in Australia that extends to the sea. Other, less-preserved goldfields can be seen in **Nelligen** and **Nerrigundah**. If you've caught the fever yourself, try your luck at fossicking for alluvial gold. With a fossicking licence and a gold pan, you can try to strike it rich at Yarramunmun Creek in Yalwal and streams around Nerriga.

🏛 Coastal History

Severs Beach has a **3500-year-old shell midden,** an indication of the eating and aquacultural practices of the Yuin people before colonisation.

Explore the area's whaling history at **Davidson Whaling Station**, by the Kiah inlet. In the 1890s the Davidson family hunted killer whales, and this weatherboard structure was where the blubber was processed. Continue the story at the **Eden Killer Whale Museum**.

Immerse yourself in the park's heritage during the multiday **Light to Light walk** or take a day trip to Green Cape Lighthouse. The history of Green Cape is often tragic, as you'll discover with the **mysterious wreck** of the *Ly-ee-Moon*.

DAMIAN PANKOWIEC/SHUTTERSTOCK ©

Keeping the Coast Afloat

THE INDUSTRIES THAT HAVE FORMED THE SOUTH COAST

Rich soil, clean ocean air and significant geological deposits have led to a multitude of industries on the South Coast. These industries have created the history and shaped the culture of the region, whether by bringing gold-mining hopefuls or providing the setting for improved equality.

Left Davidson Whaling Station (p115)
Middle Dairy cows **Right** Fishing fleet, Eden

Whaling

Whales were very important to the Dharawal and Yuin peoples. Many rock carvings along the East Coast depict whale feasts and the specific role of orcas in the Dreaming. There is evidence that Yuin people around Twofold Bay worked with orcas to beach right whales. The whales' meat was eaten, and their bones were used for water vessels and shelters.

Begun in Twofold Bay by Thomas Raine in 1828, whaling was Australia's first primary industry. Whale blubber was processed for lamp fuel and as a base for perfume or soap, and baleen (whalebone) was used for corset boning and umbrella ribbing. Whaling declined in the 1840s due to gold rushes and the petroleum industry, but the Davidson family continued to hunt wales from 1857 to the 1920s. In 1979 whaling was outlawed entirely, and now the area's cetacean-based industry is whale watching.

Gold

Gold was first found in Australia in 1851, and by the late 1850s alluvial gold had been found in the South Coast region. Scores of people flocked here, hoping to make their fortune in pickaxe mining and fossicking. However, the gold rushes in places like Bermagui and the Shoalhaven area were short-lived, rarely lasting more than three years. By 1870 the region's gold rushes were over, but some pockets of industrial gold mining were active until the 1930s. Hobbyist fossickers still frequent the streams of Shoalhaven, though they tend to find themselves richer in friendship than in gold.

Dairy

The regular rain, plentiful rivers and sheltering mountains make the South Coast very appealing to dairy farmers, who can be assured of fresh grass for their herds. Sir Thomas Sutcliffe Mort started Bodalla's first dairy in the 1860s, and his vision bloomed into a thriving industry that continues in the region today. From large-scale dairy farms supplying the entire country to micro-dairies focusing on fresh-from-the-farm tastes, the South Coast is vital in Australia's milk production.

> Many rock carvings along the East Coast depict whale feasts and the specific role of orcas in the Dreaming.

Maritime Industry

The South Coast naturally attracted maritime industries, from shipping to industrial fishing. Many of these ports are still active, such as Eden, Australia's largest industrial fishing port, and Port Kembla, a key import terminal. Lighthouses were key in marking out the often treacherous parts of the coastline. In the 19th century Wreck Bay was infamous for trapping ships too close to the coast. Between 1805 and 1928, 26 ships were wrecked around Jervis Bay, including convict ship the *Hive*.

The docks were known for their strong union presence. In 1964 the South Coast Aboriginal Advancement League worked with the Maritime Union to enforce a series of supply bans to local segregated stores. Stores were thus forced to serve Aboriginal customers, leading to desegregation along much of the South Coast years before the official change in the law.

ⓘ Oysters Through the Years

Oysters formed a key part of the diets of Indigenous peoples on the South Coast, as evidenced by the prevalence of oyster shells in numerous middens. Oysters were in high demand from the early 1800s, both for their meat and for their shells, the latter a source of lime for cement production. Harvesting depleted natural oyster deposits, so commercial farming began in the 1870s. The industry peaked in the 1970s, during which time more than 150 million Sydney rock oysters were produced across the country. Today, oyster production is Australia's most lucrative aquaculture industry.

Listings

BEST OF THE REST

Taproom Stars

Dangerous Ales $

This place in Milton has been making bold moves ever since it started. Expect more than a standard lager.

Flamin Galah Brewing Co $$

Loved, frequented and founded by Jervis Bay locals, this brewpub opened its doors in 2021.

Jervis Bay Brewing Co. $

The Bay's first craft brewery is favoured for its bright, beachy brews.

Bulli Brewing Co. $$

An eco-conscious, IPA-driven venture in Unanderra helmed by a mad-genius head brewer.

Reub Goldberg Brewing Machine $$

A custom-built brew machine, Swap n Go Growlers, and German-inspired brews. In Tarrawanna.

Coal Coast Brewing $

Aims to reflect the untameable South Coast with its down-to-earth beers.

South Coast Distillery $$

Instantly recognisable by its wave-shaped bottle and acclaimed mix of bold botanicals.

Headlands Distilling Co. $$$

This place keeps its spirits close to its heart, with a grain-to-glass philosophy and locally inspired infusions.

Tara Distillery $$

Draws inspiration from the sea for its sea-lettuce-infused gin, and from its Irish heritage for Australia's first legal *poitín*. In Jervis Bay.

North of Eden $$$

A Stony Creek micro-distillery producing intricately crafted gins, with only 200 bottles per batch.

Seaside Snacks

Rick Stein at Bannisters $$$

Shutterstocked with kickstarting the South Coast's food culture, Bannisters in Mollymook is a luxurious treat with top-quality seafood.

Nowra Fresh Fish & Farmers Market $

Fresh produce, great fish and chips, and amazing deli produce, all in one location.

Gunyah $$

In Huskisson, enjoy modern dining among the treetops, with possums and sugar gliders for dinner company.

Dog & Monocle $$

Trendy steampunk-inspired Nowra restaurant with a cosy, romantic vibe.

Pilgrims Café $$

A vegetarian institution loved by Milton locals for decades. Try the Bliss Burger!

Coolangatta Estate

Small Town Food & Wine $$

A cosy, kitchen-bench atmosphere, highlighting the amazing food and wine of the region. In Milton.

Queen St Eatery $$

A casual and welcoming, French-inspired bistro in Berry with plenty of seafood on offer.

Berry Doughnut Van $

Beloved by locals and visitors alike, these sweet treats are a great reason to stop in Berry.

Milk Haus $$

Seasonal, farm-to-table meals, grown in the restaurant garden.

Mossy Café $

Modern cafe fare within the walls of Mossy Point's original 1939 general store.

Little Prince $$

A trendy laneway-style cocktail bar in Wollongong championing spirits of the South Coast.

From Aubin to Zinfandel

Cambewarra Estate $$

A sunny, second-generation winery with a cellar door, high tea and a restaurant.

Coolangatta Estate $$$

Famed for its reds, this winery is situated in original convict-built cottages.

Crooked River Wines $$$

Regularly hosts events and festivals on its property overlooking the beautiful Gerringong area.

Lyrebird Ridge $$

Makes certified organic wines and ports, taking its name from the lyrebirds heard across the property.

Mountain Ridge Wines $$

An impressive range of wines and liqueurs.

Greenfield Beach

Tilba Valley Winery $$

Overlooks Corunna Lake and produces traditional grape varieties such as semillon and cabernet sauvignon.

Elysium Wines $$

Focuses on fruit and dessert wines incorporating native fruits like lilly-pilly and lemon aspen.

Sun, Sea & Sand

City Beach

A stone's throw from central Wollongong, this beach is perfect for an afternoon dip before dinner at a nearby cocktail bar.

Port Kembla Beach

Come for the Olympic-size ocean pool, stay for the quirky 1912 changing sheds.

Werri Beach

An expansive beach in Gerringong with a swimming lagoon at one end.

Seven Mile Beach

You'll always be able to find your own spot on the sand along this seemingly endless Shoalhaven Heads beach.

Greenfield Beach

One of Jervis Bay's many beaches, Greenfield has pure white sand and water that's clear enough to see the ocean floor.

Cabbage Tree Beach

This quiet bay beach is great for ocean swimming, with local wildlife as your only company. In Jervis Bay.

Callala Beach

Still waters make for a tranquil visit, or an ideal location for kayaking and paddleboarding. In Jervis Bay.

Green Patch Beach

Boasts mint-green waters, which you can explore on your own in this secluded Jervis Bay location.

Mollymook Beach

White-sand beach particularly popular with visiting families.

Tomakin Cove

Sheltered bay beach granting gentle waves perfect for ocean swimming.

Pebbly Beach

Friendly kangaroos frequent this beach in Murramarang National Park, with nary a pebble in sight.

Blue Pool

Swim in the azure waters of this acclaimed rock pool in Bermagui.

Natural Wonders

Cathedral Rocks

These distinctive rocks in Kiama have eroded in the shape of a church steeple.

Glasshouse Rocks

More than 400 years older than the Twelve Apostles, these towering formations in Narooma are couched among pillow lava.

The Pinnacles

These magnificent dichromatic cliffs are composed of white sands and red clay. In the Pambula-Haycock area.

Horse Head Rock

One of the oldest rocks in NSW, this regal Bermagui formation is best viewed at low tide.

Australia Rock

Snap a photo through this rock that has worn down in the shape of Australia. In Narooma.

Museums & More

Wollongong Art Museum

Sets the standard for regional art museums, with an impressive collection of modern Aboriginal art.

Bulli Black Diamond Museum

Shares the stories of the area's coal-mining heritage, as well as the history of Bulli.

Meroogal

This stunning example of 1880s Carpenter Gothic is now preserved as a house museum. In Nowra.

Jervis Bay Maritime Museum

Showcases historical boats from the region and regularly hosts art exhibitions.

Mogo Zoo

Houses more than 200 animals from 30 species in an expansive African savannah environment.

Cathedral Rocks

Ulladulla Fossil House
Fossils from Ulladulla and beyond are displayed in the area's oldest building.

Eden Killer Whale Museum
Explores the great importance of the orca to the Aboriginal people and settlers of Eden.

Oysters from the Shellardoor

Narooma Bridge Seafoods
Just off the Princes Hwy, this humble beach shack serves fresh-as-fresh oysters, prawns, fish and lobsters.

Wapengo Rocks Organic Oysters
Certified organic. Call ahead so you can fill your Esky guilt free.

Tathra Oysters
Open November to June, Tathra Oysters supplies many high-end Sydney restaurants.

Wonboyn Rock Oysters
These sweet and creamy oysters are farmed in a remote section of Wonboyn Lake.

Merimbula Gourmet Oysters
This place farms the native Sydney rock and Angasi oysters.

Wheelers
Runs tours of its farm at 11am daily, which of course involves tasting the product. It also has an attached seafood restaurant.

Outdoor Adventures Galore

Pam Burridge Surf School
Run by former surfing world champion Pam Burridge, who teaches paddleboarding as well as surfing.

SkySurf Paragliding
As you enter Wollongong you might see paragliders on the horizon. Join their ranks and enjoy a bird's-eye view of the coast.

Eden Killer Whale Museum

Hangglide Oz
Soar from the cliffs of Stanwell Park and Wollongong for this memorable experience.

Skydive Australia
Offers a tandem dive over Wollongong's central beach, landing near North Gong Beach.

Otford Farm Horse Riding
Live your bushranger fantasy as you ride through Australian bushland.

Illawarra Surf Academy
Offers lessons for surfers of all levels, focusing on getting you out in the water and having fun.

Woebegone FreeDive
Living in Huskisson for 15 years, the duo who runs this outfit offers snorkelling and free-dive tours of the area.

Crest Diving
Experiences for divers of all experience levels in the crystal-clear waters of Jervis Bay.

Windang Diving & Spearfishing
Prepare with beginner courses, or train in specialised skills, such as wreck diving.

 Scan to find more things to do in South Coast NSW online

20 Seeking Cultural
INSIGHT

TRADITION | CULTURE | SPIRITUALITY

▬▬▬ Australia is home to hundreds of Aboriginal nations, with rich and diverse cultural practices. The perspective of Australia's First Nations peoples will change the way you view the country, and allow you to travel to the different nations that make up this land.

C PROUD/TEQ & SPIRITS OF THE RED SAND ©

How to

Where am I? Find what Aboriginal nation you are visiting with the Aiatsis *Map of Australia* or gambay.com.au/languages.

Weather patterns Aboriginal peoples have different calendars to the Western one, which more accurately describe the local seasons.

Bush tucker Many botanical gardens grow native plants, and may offer interactive tasting tours.

Faboriginal The Art Gallery of NSW was the set of this TV game show testing celebrities' knowledge of Aboriginal art.

EQROY/SHUTTERSTOCK ©

SIDE TRIP SEEKING CULTURAL INSIGHT

Life Before Colonisation

At **Spirits of the Red Sand** visitors can see a recreated Aboriginal village as it would have been before European contact. Inspired by similar projects by Maori communities in New Zealand, Uncle Eddie Ruska and his family set up this experience in Beenleigh, on beautiful Yugambeh Country.

Their acclaimed evening performance runs from the Dreaming through to European contact. Live theatre and traditional song and dance work together to bring the past to life, delivering significant truths about this country's Indigenous peoples.

During the day, Elders welcome visitors to their land at the Welcome to Country cultural experience. In this interactive performance, visitors witness a smoking ceremony, learn about and deliver a message stick, enjoy a

KEITMA/SHUTTERSTOCK ©

Take a Tour

On Stradbroke Island, Quandamooka Coast runs the country's only Indigenous-owned whale-watching tours. You can learn about Eora bush food in Sydney's Botanic Gardens. Melbourne's Royal Botanic Gardens are a significant cultural site, and Indigenous guides will explain the area's importance to the people of the Kulin nation.

Left Royal Botanic Gardens, Melbourne **Above left** Traditional dance, Spirits of the Red Sand **Above right** Australian Institute of Aboriginal and Torres Strait Islander Studies (Aiatsis), Canberra

bush-tucker tasting, participate in boomerang painting and weaponry demonstrations, and feel the continuing strength of Indigenous culture. You can also explore the replica 1800s colonial township, consisting of 20 buildings frozen in time at the meeting point of Western and Aboriginal cultures.

Traditional & Modern Art

Whether it be an example of traditional techniques or an expression of strength and resistance, Indigenous art is as beautiful as it is unique. Many Australian museums have collections of both traditional and contemporary work. Queensland Art Gallery and Gallery of Modern Art has significant collections of contemporary Aboriginal and Torres Strait Islander art.

Yuin Culture Immersion

Rather than simply learning about Aboriginal heritage, the **Ngaran Ngaran Culture Awareness** retreat invites you to engage with and experience Yuin culture. Dwayne Barron-

Indigenous Wares & Fare

Sydney's **Blak Markets** provide a space for Indigenous-owned small businesses to promote and sell their products. The markets are more than just a place to shop: there are smoking ceremonies, dance and music, as well as a wonderful community atmosphere drawing Aboriginal people from all over Sydney.

Mabu Mabu Tuck Shop is located on the land of the Boonwurrung and Wurundjeri peoples in the Melbourne suburb of Yarraville. Owned by Torres Strait Islander woman Nornie Bero, the Mabu Mabu mission is to make native ingredients accessible and popular.

Left Yuin Retreat Far left Mabu
Mabu's native-ingredient products
Below Experience performers, Spirits
of the Red Sand

Harrison, a Yuin-Ngarrugu man, founded the retreat to maintain and strengthen connections to traditional Yuin culture. You'll get the most out of your visit if you arrive with respect and genuine curiosity. Guests are invited to walk with Dwayne and his family to experience traditional language, values, food and culture. Dwayne shares his culture with knowledge, passion and generosity.

First, you are invited to take part in a smoking ceremony, cleansing you of bad spirits and giving you the purest possible experience on Yuin Country. Over the course of the following 40 hours, you will experience music, dance and storytelling. You will learn about the spirits and stories that inhabit the land you stand on, and you will try bush food and bush medicine used by the Yuin people for millennia. Overnight accommodation in bell tents or private cabins is included as you travel. All meals are provided, featuring products from Mirritya Mundya Indigenous Twist.

The two-night retreat is not just a tour. It is an experience where you will immerse yourself in Indigenous culture. Previous guests speak of seeing the country in a new light and finding peace and spirituality in places they hadn't before. The Yuin retreat is a gift, and a unique insight into one of the oldest living cultures on Earth.

Australia's First Nations People

CUSTODIANS OF THE EARTH'S OLDEST CONTINUOUS CULTURE

Indigenous Australian culture dates back at least 60,000 years. Prior to European invasion in 1788, there were approximately 300 distinct language groups and 500 dialects. Now, Indigenous peoples make up only 3% of the population. Most Indigenous people live in urban areas, though some communities maintain traditional lifestyles in remote regions.

Left Invasion Day protesters **Middle** Quandong fruit **Right** Ice cream made with indigenous ingredients

HOLLI/SHUTTERSTOCK ©

Walking the Dreaming

Aboriginal culture and spirituality revolve around Dreaming and Dreamtime. The Dreamtime tells us about how things came to be. It details the creation of the natural world – rivers, mountains, plants, animals, and everything in between.

The Dreaming explains why things are the way they are, such as the birth of the first platypus, how the echidna got her spines, or the meanings of certain constellations. The Dreaming is always occurring, without a defined beginning or end. It tells us about how we should behave, about our culture and families, and about living from and respecting the land.

Dreamtime and Dreaming stories differ across nations, though some nations share the same or similar stories. These stories have been passed down through oral storytelling, dance and art, and now many stories have also been written down.

An important part of the Dreaming is that Aboriginal people are the custodians, not the owners, of the land they live on. Instead, the relationship between the land and the people is a reciprocal one, where we care for the land because it cares for us.

Many of these Dreaming stories are connected to songlines, which are paths walked by the spirits in the Dreamtime. Songlines serve many purposes, such as preserving history, detailing agricultural practices and mapping the land.

DAVIDSON PLUM

Living off the Land

For many years it was assumed that Indigenous peoples were hunter-gatherer societies prior to invasion. However, Aboriginal testimonies and recent historical research indicate that Indigenous societies employed complex aquaculture and agriculture practices. Structures such as weirs and dams still exist, and agricultural techniques and knowledges are being revived and passed on.

> The Dreaming tells us about how we should behave, about our culture and families, and about living from and respecting the land.

Many Aboriginal communities recognise different seasons from the ones in the Western calendar. These seasons usually align with the area's weather patterns or relate to the local flora and fauna. The Wurundjeri people of Victoria recognise seven seasons, such as Biderap, which is sunny and dry, and Warin, when the wombat and the moth are by the creek. Understanding the Indigenous calendar in the area you are visiting may help you better prepare for the specific weather of the region. Knowing when to dress for the hot and windy, the wet and windy, or the cool and dry can make a big difference to your enjoyment of your travels.

Bush tucker (food) and bush medicine are still used today. Some bush tucker, such as pepperberries, quandongs and Davidson plums, is used in fusion cooking and can be found in restaurants.

ⓘ The Difficult Date

The date 26 January, when the First Fleet of settlers arrived at Sydney Cove in 1788, officially become Australia Day in 1948. For Aboriginal peoples, 26 January is a more sombre occasion, marking the beginning of invasion, seizure of the land and erosion of our culture. It is referred to as the Day of Mourning, Survival Day or Invasion Day. For many Indigenous people and their supporters, Invasion Day is a day of remembrance and resistance rather than celebration. The issue is contentious in Australia, and calls to keep or change the date occur every year.

Countries, Clans & Cousins

Individual clans exist within Aboriginal nations. Clans within the same language group usually speak dialects that are mutually intelligible. Within these clans are individual families, though Aboriginal families integrate the extended family more than most Western societies do. In some communities it is common to refer to your mother's sister as Mum rather than Aunty, and to call your first cousins your brother- or sister-cousins. Some people may use 'cousin' to refer to anyone within their clan, skin group or language group. 'Cuz' is also a term of affection among Aboriginal people even if they are from completely different nations.

> Family and community ties are vital to Aboriginal culture. Your family tells you who you are and where you come from.

Family and community ties are vital to Aboriginal culture. Your family tells you who you are and where you come from. Many nations identify family ties by plant and animal totems. It is common to have your personal totem plus three further totems indicating your nation, your clan and your family ties. Sadly, much of this information has been lost, and it is a difficult journey for some people to find their family totems.

Aboriginal People Today

Across Australia, it is estimated that only 75 Indigenous languages are still spoken, but there are continuing efforts to revive languages among Indigenous communities. It is now possible to listen to music, watch TV shows or take classes in a number of Aboriginal languages. Aboriginal words are also present in the Australian vernacular. Animals such as koalas, dingoes, barramundi and galahs derive their names from Aboriginal languages, as do billabongs and boogie boards.

Similarly, Aboriginal words from different communities have spread through Australian Aboriginal English, the dialect of English spoken by many Aboriginal people across the country.

Around 60% of Aboriginal people in Australia live on the East Coast. This will sometimes surprise visitors to Australia, who think that they do not see many Aboriginal people in the region. Others are confused when a light-skinned person identifies as Aboriginal. It is widely accepted among Aboriginal communities that your percentage of Aboriginality has little bearing on your identity and involvement in the community. People with light skin and

blonde hair will proudly call themselves Blak or identify as Blackfullas. A common metaphor is that of a cup of tea: no matter how much milk you put in the cup, no matter how pale it becomes, it's still tea.

This also means that a lot of Aboriginal people live off-Country, meaning that they live on the land of another nation.

Since 1975 the first Sunday of July has marked the beginning of Naidoc Week, which is dedicated to celebrating Aboriginal culture, history and perseverance. Communities, cities, schools and other institutions hold events that celebrate and build awareness about the rich and diverse Aboriginal cultures in Australia today.

Sorry Day (8 February) commemorates the day the Australian government formally apologised for its role in the Stolen Generations. From 1910 to the 1970s, Aboriginal children were forcibly removed from their families to integrate them into white society. Aboriginal people today still feel the effects of this policy through loss of culture, family ties and language. The apology was given in 2008.

Signs of Respect

An Acknowledgement of Country and a Welcome to Country are important statements that identify and thank the custodians of the land on which an event takes place. Anyone, Aboriginal or not, can give an Acknowledgement. Welcomes can only be given by Elders from that country, or a member of the community who has been given permission by their Elders.

Elders and cultural teachers are usually referred to with 'Aunty' or 'Uncle' before their first name, in the same way that respect is conferred by the use of 'Sir' or 'Ma'am'. This recognises the knowledge and experience that our Elders hold.

Far left Boomerang carving lesson **Left** Aboriginal tools and weapons **Above left** Koomurri Dance Group Naidoc Week, Sydney **Above right** Australian and Aboriginal flags, Sorry Day, Sydney

MELBOURNE

CULTURE | HISTORY | FEASTING

Experience Melbourne online

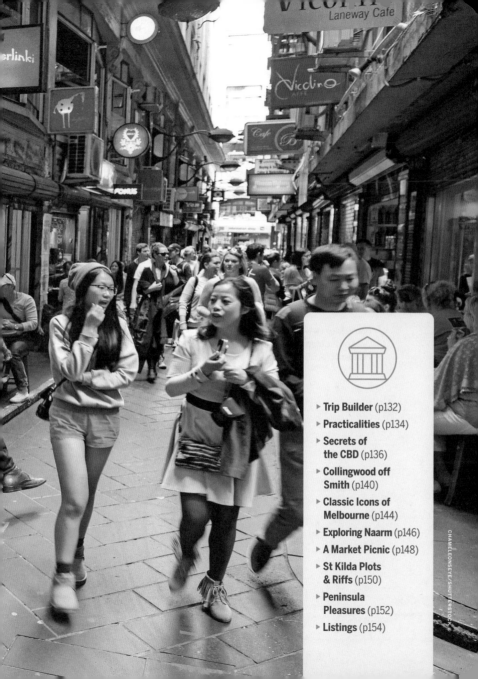

MELBOURNE
Trip Builder

Forget blockbuster beaches and endless
sunshine: Melbourne's beauty is deeper and more
complex. This is Australia's most cultured metropolis,
an electrifying mix of razor-sharp art, design and
dining, extraordinary architecture, sculpture-graced
wineries and moody coastal landscapes made for
long, pensive wanders.

Be moved at
the **Bunjilaka
Aboriginal Cultural
Centre** (p147)
🕐 *2 hours*

Stumble upon
studios and
offbeat shops
in the **Nicholas
Building** (p138)
🕐 *2 hours*

Hop between waves and
vines on the **Mornington
Peninsula** (p152)
🕐 *1 day*

PORT
MELBOURNE

Inset

*Port
Phillip*

*Western
Port*

*Port
Phillip*

MORNINGTON
PENINSULA

PHILLIP
ISLAND

0 ——— 10 km
0 ——— 5 miles

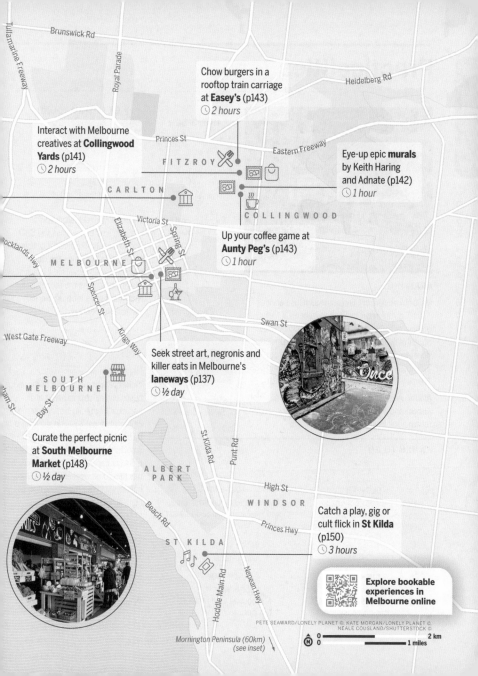

Chow burgers in a rooftop train carriage at **Easey's** (p143)
🕐 2 hours

Interact with Melbourne creatives at **Collingwood Yards** (p141)
🕐 2 hours

Eye-up epic **murals** by Keith Haring and Adnate (p142)
🕐 1 hour

Up your coffee game at **Aunty Peg's** (p143)
🕐 1 hour

Seek street art, negronis and killer eats in Melbourne's **laneways** (p137)
🕐 ½ day

Curate the perfect picnic at **South Melbourne Market** (p148)
🕐 ½ day

Catch a play, gig or cult flick in **St Kilda** (p150)
🕐 3 hours

Explore bookable experiences in Melbourne online

Brunswick Rd

Heidelberg Rd

Tullamarine Freeway

Royal Parade

Princes St

Eastern Freeway

FITZROY

CARLTON

COLLINGWOOD

Victoria St

Elizabeth St

Spring St

MELBOURNE

Docklands Hwy

Spencer St

Kings Way

Swan St

West Gate Freeway

SOUTH MELBOURNE

Bay St

St Kilda Rd

Punt Rd

ALBERT PARK

High St

WINDSOR

Beach Rd

Princes Hwy

ST KILDA

Hoddle Main Rd

Nepean Hwy

Mornington Peninsula (60km) (see inset)

Ⓝ 0 — 2 km
0 — 1 miles

Practicalities

SHUANG LI/SHUTTERSTOCK ©

ARRIVING

Melbourne Airport Frequent SkyBus services reach Southern Cross Station in central Melbourne, with additional services to Docklands, Southbank and St Kilda. A one-way/return adult ticket to Southern Cross Station costs from $15/28. A taxi to the city costs from around $55. Journey time is around 25 minutes for both.

Avalon Airport SkyBus also runs between Avalon Airport and Southern Cross Station. A one-way/return adult ticket costs from $24/45.

HOW MUCH FOR A

Piccolo (coffee) $4.50

Wood-fired pizza $20–30

Gig at Northcote Social Club $30

GETTING AROUND

Trams & trains Melbourne's iconic trams criss-cross the CBD and extend through most of the inner suburbs. Trains are the fastest way to travel significant distances across the metro area, with most lines looping around central Melbourne.

Tickets & passes Trams, trains and buses use electronic myki cards, available from train stations, some city tram stops, 7-Eleven stores and by using Google Pay on Android smartphones. A two-hour adult fare is $4.60, capped at $9.20 for the day ($6.70 on weekends and public holidays). A Free Tram Zone covers central Melbourne.

Driving A car is handy for day trips to surrounding regions, including the Mornington Peninsula and Yarra Valley.

WHEN TO GO

DEC–FEB
Hot days and cool changes, music festivals, outdoor cinema and Grand Slam tennis

MAR–MAY
Mild weather, golden foliage and the Melbourne Food and Wine Festival

JUN–AUG
Chilly days made for museums and galleries, AFL matches and cosy pubs

SEP–NOV
Footy-finals fever, Melbourne Cup fashion, temperamental weather

EATING & DRINKING

Beyond Melbourne's celeb-chef restaurants is a wealth of casual, affordable eateries serving authentic global cuisines. Hit Chinatown and Swanston St (city centre) for East Asian, Carlton for Italian, Brunswick and Coburg for Middle Eastern, North Richmond for Vietnamese, and Footscray (pictured top) for Vietnamese and Ethiopian.

The Melbourne region claims some top gin distilleries, including Four Pillars, voted 'World's Best' several years running. Other noteworthy makers include Melbourne Gin Company and Brogan's Way (pictured bottom).

Best wine bar
Marion (p156)

Must-try
Vegemite curry buttermilk roti at Sunda (p157)

CONNECT & FIND YOUR WAY

Wi-fi Free hotspots in central Melbourne include Bourke St Mall, Queen Victoria Market and Melbourne Museum; select VicFreeWiFi. Free wi-fi is common at libraries, museums, cafes and apartment rentals. Some hostels and hotels still charge.

Navigation Melbourne's largely grid-style road system makes navigation straightforward. If driving, consider that some narrower inner-city streets are one way.

WHERE TO STAY

Book well ahead if your trip coincides with major events like the Australian Open, Formula 1 Grand Prix and Melbourne Cup.

Neighbourhood	Atmosphere
City Centre (CBD) & Southbank	World-class cultural sights, shopping, dining and entertainment. Noisy.
Carlton, Fitzroy & Collingwood	Victorian-era architecture, vibrant dining, arts and nightlife, interesting shops.
Brunswick & Northcote	Further out, but Melbourne's hipster heartland. Great bars and live-music venues.
South Yarra, Prahran & Windsor	Fashionable and sceney; Windsor coolest. Buzzing eateries, bars and clubs.
St Kilda	Cosmopolitan beachside neighbourhood. Seedy in parts.

FOUR SEASONS IN ONE DAY

Melbourne's weather is infamously erratic. Bring layers of clothes you can peel off or slip on as required throughout the day.

MONEY

Buy picnic provisions at markets, delis and supermarkets. Vietnamese takeaway restaurants serve fresh, cheap grub.

Halftix (halftixmelbourne.com) offers discounted theatre tickets, including to blockbuster musicals and Melbourne Theatre Company productions. Also check out www.todaytix.com.

21

Secrets of
THE CBD

CREATIVITY | ARCHITECTURE | FOOD

Melbourne's CBD (Central Business District) holds its cards close to its chest. Here, laneways and unassuming doors lead to impeccably curated galleries and shops, architectural wonders, and rooftop drinks with sucker-punch views. Lace up your coolest kicks and seek out the city's finest assets.

JAKE RODEN ©

🗺 How to

Getting around The CBD is relatively compact and best explored on foot. Free city trams are a handy backup.

When to go Some shops don't open before 11am and some office buildings are closed on weekends, so consider exploring on a weekday afternoon. Note that some businesses close for several weeks in January.

Melbourne Street Tours Three-hour explorations of the city's dynamic street-art scene, as well as street-art workshops. Book online.

TONKA ©

Down the Laneways

Degraves St, Centre Pl, Hardware Lane and graffiti-drenched Hosier Lane may be the CBD's most Insta-famous laneways, but other alleyways harbour exceptional finds. On Presgrave Lane, tiny **Bar Americano** pours exceptional negronis, while nondescript Watson Pl harbours **Craft Victoria**, a gallery-store championing local makers. Relics from an infamous slum punctuate Casselden Pl, where a 19th-century brothel (the only single-storey house left in the CBD) is now **Little Lon Distilling**, an intimate cocktail bar offering gin masterclasses. Excellent eateries and bars dot Crossley and Liverpool Sts, while gritty Duckboard Place claims Steen Jones' soaring 'Melbourne' mural, exceptional Chinese eatery **Lee Ho Fook** and new-school Indian **Tonka** (order the *pani puri*).

PARKER BLAIN ©

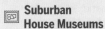

Suburban House Museums

While the National Gallery of Victoria is a must for culture vultures, consider booking a guided tour of **Lyon Housemuseum** or **Justin Art House Museum**. Located in suburbia, both showcase private collections of contemporary art, exhibited in the collectors' covetable homes.

Left Yum cha brunch, Lee Ho Fook **Above left** Little Lon Distilling **Above Right** Indian dish, Tonka

Vertical Villages

Step out of the laneways and into Melbourne's 'vertical villages': early-20th-century buildings stacked floor upon floor with independent galleries, eateries, bars and more. Legendary artist and muse Vali Myers had her studio in Swanston St's **Nicholas Building**, where subway-tiled corridors lead to one-off enterprises peddling everything from local millinery to vintage Manolo Blahnik slingbacks. Directly above the building's leadlight arcade, Flinders Lane Gallery showcases the work of Australian artists. You could spend all afternoon and evening in art nouveau **Curtin House**, shopping niche streetwear at unisex PAM, leafing through design tomes at Metropolis Bookshop, or downing cocktails and jungle curry at Cookie. Hit the rooftop bar for skyscraper views (and seasonal rooftop cinema), and always check the line-up at the Toff. The Toff's Orient Express–style private booths are hot property; book ahead to secure one.

✅ Simone's Picks

The **Capitol** is a spectacular art deco theatre. Designed by Marion Mahony Griffin and Walter Burley Griffin, it has a flamboyantly geometric ceiling and hosts interesting cultural events. In **Guildford Lane**, residents and businesses have populated their doorstops and balconies with potted plants, turning the street into a little oasis. At the rear of NGV International, the magical **Grollo Equiset Garden** hosts the gallery's annual Architecture Commission and comes alive over the summer months. Lastly, floating, open-air bar **Ponyfish Island** is perfect for watching boats motor by.

■ **Tips by Simone LeAmon,**
Hugh DT Williamson Curator of Contemporary Design and Architecture at the National Gallery of Victoria
@simoneleamon

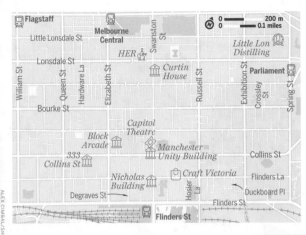

Left Capitol theatre interior **Below** 333 Collins St interior

On Lonsdale St, one-time cigarette factory Pacific House is now **Her**, a four-level culinary destination whose offerings include a smoky Thai eatery and a Japanese-inspired listening bar.

Hidden Wonders of Collins Street

On prestigious Collins St, architectural highlights often lie hidden in plain sight. Take **333 Collins St**, a Gotham-esque 1990s office building built over a spectacular domed banking chamber from the 1890s. Across the street, the ornate exterior of the **ANZ Bank** (1883–87) hints at the Venetian-inspired opulence inside. After fawning over the banking hall's 23-carat gold-leaf detailing, head through the doors at the rear to reach the stained-glass Cathedral Room. At mosaicked **Block Arcade** (1893), many miss Phillip Goatcher's allegorical ceiling painting (1907) in the L'Occitane store. On the northeast corner of Collins and Swanston Sts, the **Manchester Unity Building** (1932) houses Victoria's first escalator and restored lifts adorned with elegant Queensland maple. Head up the escalator to peek at what was once a glamorous art deco shopping arcade; press the buzzer to enter and head along the arcade to exit to the lifts. Monthly building tours (manchesterunitybuilding.com.au) include access to the rooftop and boardroom, the latter an internationally renowned deco masterpiece; the afternoon 'Wine and Cheese Tour' is best.

22 Collingwood off
SMITH

CREATIVITY | COFFEE | BEER

▰▰▰▰ Once infamous for sooty factories and toothless footy-club supporters, gentrifying Collingwood fizzes with dynamic creativity and enterprise. Veer east of its of-the-moment dining-and-retail strip Smith St to discover skyscraping street art, heritage-listed quirks, and some bloody good beer and coffee to boot.

How to

Getting here From the CBD it's a 15- to 20-minute ride on tram 86.

When to go Later in the week is best, with Saturday afternoons especially good for a friendly and buzzy neighbourhood vibe.

Classic dives Hazy Collingwood memories are made rocking out at indie-music pub the Tote or queer club the Peel (aka the 'Squeal').

Going Japanese Brunch on *tamagoyaki* at factory-turned-cafe-store Cibi or book a traditional Japanese bathing experience at Ofuroya.

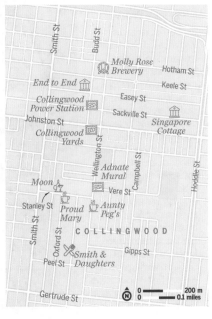

Doing the Yards

A 6500-sq-metre precinct of studios and galleries, community radio stations, one-off shops, bars and some of Australia's leading artist-run initiatives, **Collingwood Yards** is a hotbed of cultural collaborations. Before heading in (try to visit Thursday to Saturday), resident artist Emily Floyd recommends checking the Bus Projects (busprojects.org. au), Westspace (westspace.org.au), Liquid Architecture (liquidarchitecture.org.au) and Agency Projects (agencyprojects.org) websites for current exhibitions, talks and performances. Artist markets are sometimes held in the courtyard, itself flanked by Social Studio, selling fashion, design and accessories by Indigenous and culturally diverse creatives; check out its atelier upstairs.

Art on the Streets

Collingwood's gritty streets are nectar for street artists. Local public-housing tenants feature in **Adnate's 20-storey mural** (corner

Left Yorkshire Brewery (p142) **Above left** Resident ceramicist Tantri Mustika, Collingwood Yards

of Wellington and Vere Sts). Stand further south on Wellington St to fully appreciate what is the tallest mural in the southern hemisphere. Adnate's work also features at **Collingwood Power Substation** (corner of Budd and Sackville Sts), alongside fellow Melbourne-based Rone. Budd St and the alleyways off it are always pimped with eye-popping works, and you'll find large-scale jaw-droppers on the side wall of nearby **46 Easey St**. Collingwood also claims one of the world's few surviving murals by American pop artist Keith Haring, painted on the side of what is now **Collingwood Yards'** Johnston St Building.

Architectural Curiosities

Down narrow Waterloo Rd lies the heritage-listed relics of the former **Yorkshire Brewery**. Among them is a polychromatic brick brew tower, designed in the Second Empire style and Melbourne's tallest building between 1867 and 1888. If the timber abode at 136

 Emily's Picks

Collingwood Yards was formerly a technical trade college where I studied. I love discovering traces of the site's material history. In the corridor outside my studio there's a beautiful blackboard used for teaching carpentry. In the leafy courtyard, **Hope St Radio** (hopestradio.community) hosts convivial gatherings; all are welcome. Yálla-birr-ang (Collingwood) has a rich history of First Peoples creative practice. For a sonic exploration, I recommend local radio station **3CR** (3cr.org.au). Favourite podcasts centring First Peoples' voices and community-led struggle include Yarra Elders Precious Memories and Thursday Breakfast Interviews.

 ■ **Emily Floyd,** *artist working in sculpture and public installation* @emilyfloyd0

⊘ Carn the Pies!

Aussie Rules Football (AFL) is Melbourne's unofficial religion and Collingwood's 'Magpies' (the 'Pies') one of its most colourful teams. While the men's team plays home games at the MCG (mcg.org.au), its spiritual home **Victoria Park** hosts Collingwood's women's team (collingwoodfc.com.au/teams/aflw).

Sackville St looks dropped straight out of vintage Asia, that's because it is. Dubbed the **Singapore Cottage**, it's a rare example of the prefabricated abodes commonly imported to Melbourne during the 1850s gold rush. Nearby, daredevil modern engineering underscores concrete office block **End to End** (48 Easey St). Designed by Collingwood's provocative ITN Architects, the building is wildly crowned by three decommissioned train carriages. One of the carriages is home to top-notch burger bar **Easey's**.

From Brunch to Brew

South of Johnston St, brunch creatively at **Proud Mary Coffee**, whose sibling **Aunty Peg's** is practically a 'cellar door' for speciality coffee (served only black); check its socials for community cupping sessions. Rock 'n' roll chef Shannon Martinez is behind plant-based restaurant **Smith & Daughters** and the more casual **Smith & Deli**, while intimate wine bar **Moon** has a rocking selection of niche vino by the glass. North of Johnston St, **Acoffee** makes flawless lattes. A few doors down, locals kick back with IPAs and ales at craft brewery the **Mill**. For an impromptu beer crawl, roll onto **Molly Rose Brewery** to slurp Nic Sandry's out-of-the-box brews.

Left Twenty-storey Adnate mural
Above top End to End office block
Above Proud Mary Coffee

CLASSIC ICONS
of Melbourne

01 Flinders Street Station clocks

If a local says 'Meet me under the clocks', they mean the row of vintage timekeepers at Flinders Street Station.

02 W-class trams

Ride one of Melbourne's historic W-class trams on the City Circle line.

03 Brighton bathing boxes

Brighton beach's brightly coloured Victorian-era bathing boxes are hot property.

In 2019, No 15 sold for a cool $340,000.

04 Melbourne Cricket Ground (MCG)

Immortalised in Paul Kelly's song 'Leaps and Bounds', the 'G' is where footy-mad Melburnians worship their burly, brawny gods.

05 Pellegrini's

It's still 1954 at this time-warped CBD espresso bar, a bastion of Italo-Melburnian life.

06 Skipping Girl

North Richmond's neon-lit Skipping Girl (Little Audrey) began life advertising vinegar in 1936.

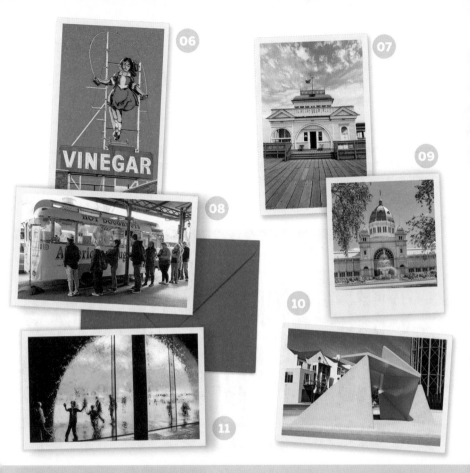

07 St Kilda Pier kiosk

St Kilda Pier's Edwardian pavilion is an architectural phoenix, rising from the ashes after burning down in 2003.

08 American Doughnut Kitchen

A trip to the Queen Vic Market isn't complete without a bag of jam-filled doughnuts from this 1950 food van.

09 Royal Exhibition Building

This World Heritage–listed show-off features a dome inspired by Brunelleschi's cupola for the Duomo in Florence.

10 Vault

Opinion was divided when Ron Robertson-Swann's abstract sculpture was unveiled in 1980. Moved twice, it now calls Southbank home.

11 National Gallery of Victoria Water Wall

Childhood memories are made of running your fingers along the NGV's trickling Water Wall.

23 Exploring
NAARM

HISTORY | CULTURE | NATURE

Melbourne's birthday cake may still be shy of 200 candles, but the land on which the city stands has sustained the Wurundjeri and Boon Wurrung people of the Kulin nation for at least 40,000 years. To its Traditional Owners, Melbourne is Naarm, and the city's bounty of Aboriginal art, stories and knowledge offers a deep connection to place as moving as it is enlightening.

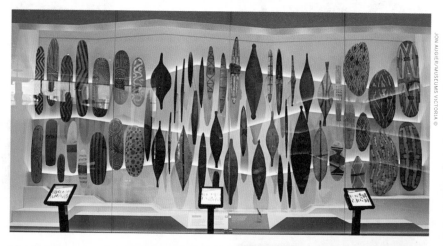

JON AUGIER/MUSEUMS VICTORIA ©

🖼 How to

Getting around Federation Sq faces Flinders Street Station. Melbourne Museum and the Royal Botanic Gardens are within walking distance of the CBD. Trams reach both.

When to go Aboriginal Melbourne can be experienced all year.

Barak Building Looking north up Swanston St from the Shrine of Remembrance, you'll notice a 31-storey, black-and-white building embedded with the face of Wurundjeri-willam artist, diplomat and *ngurungaeta* (clan leader) William Barak (1824–1903).

KIRA KIRA ANG/SHUTTERSTOCK ©

Far left top Display cases of Indigenous artefacts in the 'Many Nations' section of the First Peoples exhibition, Bunjilaka, Melbourne Museum **Far left bottom** Ian Potter Centre

Journey through time The evocative Bunjilaka Aboriginal Cultural Centre at **Melbourne Museum** explores many facets of Victoria's oldest living cultures. Learn about the art of possum-skin cloaks and the ingenuity of Budj Bim's ancient aquaculture system, listen to traditional songs of mourning, and reflect on Victoria's frontier wars. From the galleries, the easily missed Milarri Garden Walk is a beautiful spot for quiet contemplation.

Art & feasting On Federation Sq, explore works by Victorian Indigenous artists at the National Gallery of Australia's **Ian Potter Centre**. According to Myles Russell-Cook, the NGV's senior curator of Indigenous art, key works include William Barak's *Ceremony* (1898), Maree Clark's *Ritual and Ceremony* (2012), Destiny Deacon's *BLAK* (2020) and Brook Andrew's *Sexy and dangerous* (1996; printed 2005). If you're peckish, stop by neighbouring **Mabu Mabu Big Esso**, a contemporary, Indigenous-owned eatery serving excellent share plates utilising native ingredients.

A walk in the park As eucalyptus-scented smoke billows from the *tarnuk* (wooden dish), Kulin nation ancestors are acknowledged and you are welcomed to Country. The sacred *tanderrum* ceremony forms part of the Royal Botanic Gardens' **Aboriginal Heritage Walk** (rbg.vic.gov.au). Tours lead visitors through Naarm's foremost public gardens to learn about local Aboriginal culture and knowledge, from the city's six seasons to medicinal bush tucker. Book online.

ⓘ **Culture Hub**

A visit to the **Koorie Heritage Trust** on Federation Sq is a must for any itinerary, offering a unique insight into Indigenous culture. Immerse yourself in our exhibitions from Victorian First Nations artists, and experience one of the largest collections of Koorie art and artefacts on permanent display. Our Aboriginal Walking Tours are led by First Nation guides and help you gain an understanding of how Melbourne's city centre has changed over time and the significance of the Birrarung (Yarra River) to the local Kulin peoples. Our shop supports local artists and craftspeople and all products sold are authentic and unique.

■ **Tom Mosby,** *CEO of the Koorie Heritage Trust* @koorie_heritage_trust_inc

24 A Market **PICNIC**

FOOD | ARCHITECTURE | OUTDOORS

▬▬▬▬ Anthony Bourdain once proclaimed that he'd rather eat in Melbourne than Paris, and nowhere are the city's gastronomic passions more evident than at its produce markets. If the weather's fine, fill your hamper at historic South Melbourne Market and spend an afternoon feasting in nearby St Vincent Gardens, surrounded by some of Melbourne's fanciest Victorian-era abodes.

MUHAMMED YASIN IRIK/SHUTTERSTOCK ©

🗺 **How to**

Getting here From the CBD, take tram 12 or 96 to the market (15 to 20 minutes).

When to go The market is open Wednesday, Friday, Saturday and Sunday. The best picnic weather is generally from October to April.

Post-prandial pleasures Stroll to Albert Park village to browse boutiques and Avenue Bookstore. Alternatively, catch the 96 tram to St Kilda for a drink at The Esplanade or beachside Pontoon.

ADAM CALAITZIS/SHUTTERSTOCK ©

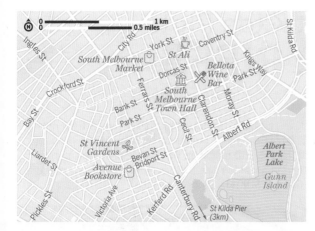

Far left top Turkish *gözleme* **Far left bottom** Market sign

Market provisions If possible, visit the market on Wednesday, when it's quieter and vendors have more time to chat. Ask questions, sample products. Bag some Spanish blue or Swiss Chällerhocker from the magnificent Cheese Room at **Emerald Deli**, and some quiche or Peter Bouchier double-smoked leg ham from **Pickadeli**. Spanish deli-bodega **La Central** has vacuum-packed Iberian smallgoods and made-to-order grazing platters. Friday to Sunday, it also sells Basque country cheesecake, often gone by lunch. The *canelés* and lemon tea cake from **Agathé Pâtisserie** are blissful, as are the house-roasted macadamias from **Nutshoppe**. Stop by **Cobb Lane** for milk rolls and by bottle shop **Swords** for some Sailors Crave craft beer or a drop from maverick Gippsland winemaker Neil Prentice (try his Holly's Garden Überbrut or Studebaker pinot).

Picnic among belles Hamper loaded, graze and laze at **St Vincent Gardens**, a neighbourhood park graced with magnolias, Moreton Bay figs and Norfolk pines. Grand 19th-century abodes – many adorned with delicate iron lacework – circle the park. Together, they form one of Australia's most beautiful heritage-listed precincts. Montague Rd divides the park in two, with the western section (home to a playground) especially appealing given its distance from busy Ferrars St. The gardens are a 1km walk from the market, a little longer if you detour via Marshall St to admire 19th-century show-off South Melbourne Town Hall.

Alejandro's Picks

My picnic essentials include *jamón* from La Central, pastries from Agathé Pâtisserie, cheese and pickles from **Steve's Deli,** and ready-to-eat seafood from **Oyster Bar by Aptus**. I also love the snacks I can eat while shopping and that I can stay for a quick breakfast or lunch. Favourite on-site market eats include dumplings from **Bambu**, traditional *gözleme* at **Köy Restaurant** and a sneaky *canelé* at Agathé Pâtisserie. Beyond the market, having coffee at **St Ali** is a great way to embrace South Melbourne's culture. **Bellota Wine Bar** is my go-to for lunch or a quiet dinner with friends.

 ■ Recommended by **Alejandro Saravia,** *executive chef and founder of Farmer's Daughters and Victoria by Farmer's Daughters* @chefalejandrosaravia

25 St Kilda Plots
& RIFFS

CULTURE | HERITAGE | COCKTAILS

▬▬▬ Postwar Jewish enclave, red-light district, punk-rocker hub, artists' muse: bayside St Kilda has always been an eclectic bohemian at heart. While property prices may be stratospheric, there's still magic on these streets, at rock 'n' roll joints, independent theatres and a Golden Age picture palace. Catch a gig, play or double feature, and let that old St Kilda energy sparkle.

GREG BALFOUR EVANS/ALAMY STOCK PHOTO ©

How to

Getting here From the CBD, trams 16 and 96 reach St Kilda (around 30 minutes). For Red Stitch and the Astor, catch a Sandringham-line train to Windsor.

When to go Year-round, but summer in St Kilda is festive.

Classic hang-outs Generations of artists have brunched, slurped coffee and scribbled down ideas at Galleon Cafe, eaten Polish cheesecake at Monarch Cakes and dined Italian-style at Cicciolina; the last has an easily missed back bar.

IGOR PRAHIN/ALAMY STOCK PHOTO ©

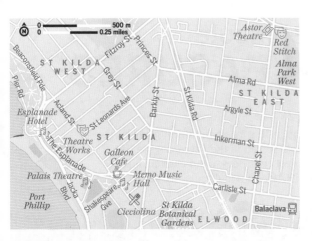

Far left top Esplanade Hotel Far left bottom Astor Theatre

Cult films in a deco landmark At night there's something deliciously noir about the softly lit lobby at the **Astor**, car lights gleaming on a rainy Chapel St outside. It might be those elegant curves, the intimate bar named after the hotel in *The Shining*, or the tinkering bell of resident feline Duke (named after John Wayne). In business since 1936, this grand old cinema has a brilliant program of cult classics and double bills, best viewed with a choc-top ice cream from the bar.

Homegrown drama Watching someone unravel is intense, especially when they're within touching distance. There are only 81 seats in the converted church hall used by **Red Stitch**, and the ensemble's productions of contemporary theatre are intelligent and powerful. These include world premieres of new Australian works, developed exclusively with the company.

Theatre Works is another platform for diverse local voices. Hankering for a contemporary circus work exploring Australia's sociopolitical landscape? You'll probably see it here.

Music at the Memo Some of the biggest names in rock, jazz, blues and electronica have played historic St Kilda venues like the Palais and the Esplanade, while the summertime St Kilda Festival – a showcase for local acts – draws massive crowds. For a more in-the-know experience, catch an act at **Memo Music Hall**, a 1920s dance hall now hosting Aussie rock and jazz legends, contemporary singer-songwriters and cabaret.

A Ghost at the Espy

Everyone who's anyone in Australian music has rocked St Kilda's **Esplanade Hotel**. Singer-songwriter Paul Kelly recorded tracks in its legendary Gershwin Room, while late Daddy Cool guitarist Ross Hannaford held a long-running residency in the front bar. Built as a seaside hotel in 1878, its guests reputedly include Mark Twain and Sarah Bernhardt. Legend has it the French actress checked in with 12 pets. These days, the Espy's best-kept secret is the Ghost of Alfred Felton, a top-floor cocktail lounge named for the art collector and philanthropist who kept rooms here until his death in 1904.

26 Peninsula
PLEASURES

BEACHES | SPAS | WINE

As good for a day trip as it is for an indulgent getaway, the Mornington Peninsula is well versed in the finer things in life, offering both wild and genteel coastlines, mind-clearing hikes and spas, stellar restaurants, wineries and sculpture gardens.

ORLOVA MARIA / ALAMY STOCK PHOTO ©

📍 Trip Notes

Getting here Hire your own car to properly explore the peninsula, a 70- to 90-minute drive south of central Melbourne.

When to go Mid-December to late January is peak season, with crowds and high prices; February to mid-March offers beach weather with thinner crowds.

Dining Book notable restaurants at least a month ahead, especially if visiting in summer and on weekends; some places only open later in the week.

✅ Top Picks

Torello Farm stocks great local produce like Cape Schanck olive oil, Main Ridge olives and sourdough bread from Mary Mother Bakes. Excellent small winery **Avani** has biodynamic estate syrah and pop-up restaurants in summer. For an interesting walk, head right of **Flinders Pier**, past the yacht club and around the cliff.

■ **Recommended by Brigitte Hafner,** *chef and owner of Tedesca Osteria* @tedesca72

05 Hop between healing mineral pools at **Peninsula Hot Springs** (pictured left), set among native tea tree. For a more luxe vibe, opt for neighbouring **Alba Thermal Springs & Spa**. Book both in advance.

04 Reserve a long, decadent lunch (or Saturday dinner) at agriturismo **Tedesca Osteria**, set in a restored farmhouse and praised for its beautiful wood-fired cooking, locavore produce and progressive wine list.

03 Quaff elegant local pinot noir and chardonnay at **Pt Leo Estate** and roam the winery's bay-facing sculpture garden, featuring large-scale contemporary pieces by renowned artists such as Jaume Plensa and Kaws.

Port Phillip

Safety Beach

Dromana

Torello Farm

McCrae

Merricks North

Rosebud

Red Hill

Mornington Peninsula Freeway

Avani

Tootgarook

Arthurs Seat State Park

Rye

Red Hill South

Dundas St

Fingal

Browns Rd

Main Ridge

Merricks

Boneo

Point Leo

St Andrews

Mornington Peninsula National Park (Greens Bush)

Shoreham

Mornington Peninsula National Park

Cape Schanck

Western Port

01 Hike the wild coast from Cape Schanck to **Bushrangers Bay** (5.2km return). If the tide is low and the weather warm, soak in the rock pools at the eastern end of the bay.

Bush-rangers Bay

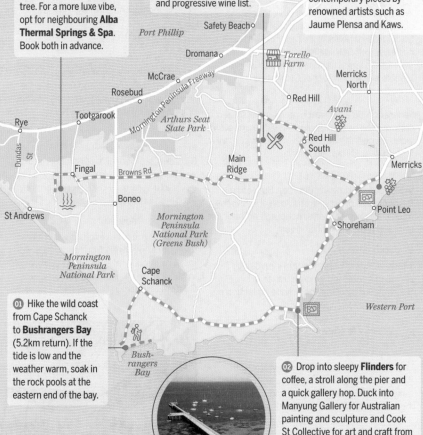

02 Drop into sleepy **Flinders** for coffee, a stroll along the pier and a quick gallery hop. Duck into Manyung Gallery for Australian painting and sculpture and Cook St Collective for art and craft from local makers.

FILEDIMAGE/SHUTTERSTOCK ©

N
0   10 km
0   5 miles

Listings

BEST OF THE REST

Old Masters, Mod Mavericks

National Gallery of Victoria (NGV): International

While the NGV's Australian collection occupies the Ian Potter Centre at Federation Sq, its international works are housed in its behemoth St Kilda Rd building, home to the world's largest stained-glass ceiling and Tiepolo's epic *Banquet of Cleopatra*.

ACMI

Federation Sq's high-tech museum of screen culture in all its forms: film, TV, video art, even video games. Dig deep at exhibitions, screenings, talks and themed festivals.

Heide Museum of Modern Art

In a bucolic setting in suburban Bulleen, the former home of art patrons John and Sunday Reed is renowned for its modernist architecture and modern Australian art.

Buxton Contemporary

Weird, wonderful and thought-provoking shows of contemporary Australian art in Southbank, featuring the private collection of avid collector Michael Buxton.

Words & Ideas

Wheeler Centre

Located at the State Library of Victoria, the Wheeler Centre runs a busy program of public talks featuring prolific minds and topics ranging from art and literature to current affairs.

La Mama

Playwriting greats including David Williamson cut their teeth at this intimate Carlton theatre, still a top spot to catch emerging local talent.

Readings

Its main Carlton branch voted World's Best Bookstore in 2016, Melbourne's favourite independent bookstore chain hosts regular book launches and talks with lauded writers.

Melbourne Tales

State Library of Victoria

One of the world's great libraries, with breathtaking heritage spaces and free galleries showcasing everything from early Melbourne paintings to bushranger Ned Kelly's armour.

Melbourne Museum

In the World Heritage–listed Carlton Gardens, Melbourne's sprawling natural- and cultural-history museum delves into the city's extraordinary backstory from refreshing perspectives.

Immigration Museum

A dynamic museum exploring identity, diversity and stories from one of the world's most multicultural societies. Suitably set in Melbourne's beautifully restored Old Customs House.

Melbourne Museum

🎵 Rocking Nights

Corner Hotel

Everyone from Ben Harper to the Dandy Warhols has played this rambunctious Richmond pub. Catch an up-and-comer or certified music legend.

Northcote Social Club

In hipster heartland Northcote, NSC is a great pub for fledgling and emerging singer-songwriters and bands, both local and touring.

Northcote Theatre

Another on-point Northcote venue, set in a restored, heritage-listed cinema dating from 1912. Bonus points for the on-site trattoria, wine bar and rooftop bar.

Cherry Bar

Noel Gallagher once offered to buy this CBD dive bar – testament to its X factor. It's a come-one-come-all joint, pumping out everything from blues and punk to retro.

JazzLab

Brunswick offspring of Melbourne's late, great jazz club Bennetts Lane, serving up top local and international sax seven nights a week.

Howler

In a Brunswick warehouse, Howler has courted the likes of British singer-songwriter SG Lewis and Aussie alt-rockers Middle Kids. Expect fresh, eclectic acts.

🏞️ Great Outdoors

Main Yarra Trail

Snaking through fragrant bushland and skirting both Collingwood Children's Farm and Heide Museum of Modern Art, this scenic, 35km cycling and walking trail connects Southbank to kangaroo-speckled Westerfolds Park.

Dandenong Ranges

Kayak Melbourne

Take in the city skyline on a guided kayaking tour along the Yarra River. Options include a sunset tour with dinner; no prior kayaking experience necessary.

Fitzroy Pool

Featured in Helen Garner's classic novel *Monkey Grip*, this historic 50m outdoor pool is more than a much-loved hang-out; it's a character in Melbourne's collective imagination.

Dandenong Ranges

These lush, cool ranges 35km east of Melbourne boast rainforest walks, elegant gardens and the thigh-busting 1000 Steps (Kokoda Track Memorial Walk).

Urbn Surf

Minutes from Melbourne Airport, Australia's first surf park rolls out wave after perfect wave, from gentle white water for rookies to 2m barrels for the next Gabriel Medina.

🛍️ Melbourne by Design

Clementine's

Affordable, locally designed and made gifts in the CBD, from Melbourne-themed totes to ceramics, contemporary jewellery, even native skincare.

Alpha60

Statement-making threads designed by two Melbourne siblings. The label's Chapter House boutique occupies a beautiful, vaulted hall by St Paul's Cathedral.

Gertrude Street

Fitzroy's hippest strip claims some of Melbourne's edgiest fashion labels, including Leonard St, Edgeley and Handsom.

Third Drawer Down

Off Gertrude St, Third Drawer Down collaborates with prolific local and international artists to create quirky, conversation-sparking homewares, gifts and accessories.

The Boroughs

A Brunswick shop celebrating Melbourne's northside creatives. Bag anything from sustainable local knitwear to leather bags, sunglasses and picture books.

Booze & Conversation

Marion $$

Sharp yet friendly staff, sophisticated small plates and out-of-the-box wines by the glass on Fitzroy's Gertrude St.

Carlton Wine Room $$

An understatedly refined Carlton favourite, complete with seasonally adjusted wine list and contemporary bites spanning grazing to mains.

Embla $$

In the CBD, congenial, intimate Embla has a New York vibe, an award-winning wine list and knockout dishes kissed by wood oven or grill.

Everleigh $$$

A hard-to-find, globally acclaimed Fitzroy heavyweight with vintage good looks and flawless, classically inspired cocktails.

Beermash $$

Laid-back and affable, Collingwood's Beermash pours a thrilling selection of craft brews, both draught and bottled. Niche ciders and wines add to the sense of adventure.

Cafe Culture

Seven Seeds $

House-roasted speciality coffee and a short, feel-good all-day menu underscore this Carlton classic, hidden up a Soho-esque side street.

Wide Open Road $

Indie vibes, comforting toasties and house-roasted beans keep northside hipsters purring at this super-local Brunswick stalwart.

Industry Beans $$

A Fitzroy-based coffee roaster revered as much for its next-level food options as for its signature blends, rotating single origins and speciality-coffee bubble cup.

Hardware Société $$

Gorgeous, Gallic-accented dishes, brunch cocktails and art by Melbourne illustrator Mads Francis, all hidden down a lesser-known CBD laneway.

Gertrude St

Foodie Hit List

Laksa King $

A casual, ever-bustling Malaysian joint in Flemington famous for its big bowls of mouth-watering laksa (spicy noodle soup).

Sunda $$

Young-gun chef Khanh Nguyen merges Southeast Asian flavours, native ingredients and new-school ingenuity to create headline-worthy dishes at his hip CBD eatery.

Anchovy $$

Critically acclaimed reinterpretations of Vietnamese cooking in Richmond. For a cheaper bite, grab a posh *bánh mi* (Vietnamese baguette sandwich) from next-door sibling Ca Com.

Savannah African Restaurant $$

Authentic Ethiopian and Eritrean home cooking in Collingwood, cooked and served by the restaurant's hospitable owner.

HuTong Dumpling Bar $$

On a CBD laneway, dexterous chefs pleat Melbourne's best *xiao long bao* (steamed dumplings filled with broth and pork). There's a second branch in Prahran.

48h Pizza e Gnocchi Bar $$

A simple menu of award-winning wood-fired pizzas, plus pillowy gnocchi and graze-friendly antipasti and olives. Two restaurant locations: South Yarra and Elsternwick.

Bowl of laksa

MELBOURNE REVIEWS

Attica $$$

Reserve months ahead to secure a table at Ben Shewry's world-famous Ripponlea restaurant, a bastion of contemporary Australian cooking at its most enlightened.

Farmer's Daughters $$$

A svelte ode to Gippsland produce in the CBD. Fine-dine in the restaurant, graze in the deli or sip updated cocktails on the rooftop. Offspring Victoria by Farmer's Daughters is a gastronomic showcase for the entire state.

Osteria Ilaria $$$

Thoughtful, modern Italo-Australian cooking in the CBD, with clever twists, house-cured meats and surprising wines.

Maha $$$

Chef Shane Delia puts an innovative spin on Middle Eastern cooking at his plush CBD restaurant. For something more casual, hit wine bar Maha East in Windsor.

Scan to find more things to do in Melbourne online

27 Great Ocean Road
EXPLORER

BEACHES | WILDLIFE | GOURMET

▬▬▬ Stretching from Torquay to Allansford, the Great Ocean Road is Australia's most fabled coastal drive, a 240km route where bracing southern waters meet luxuriant forests, emerald fields and salty beach towns. Stay awhile and let its secrets, legends and flavours bewitch you.

🗺 How to

Getting here The route's eastern gateway is Torquay, 105km southwest of Melbourne via the M1. Rent a car for maximum freedom.

When to go February–March is warm, with fewer crowds than December–January. Winter is whale-watching season.

Go west Drive from the east for the best views and easy access to lookouts.

Accommodation Book well ahead in summer, at Easter and in school-holiday periods, especially in Lorne, Anglesea and Apollo Bay.

Forest Secrets

Much of the Great Ocean Road lies within **Great Otway National Park**, which sprawls from Torquay to Princetown and north through the Otway Ranges in a sweep of rugged beaches, lush fern gullies and towering mountain ash. While some of its highlights are well known – koala spotting in **Kennett River**, hiking to **Hopetoun Falls** (especially beautiful in late winter and spring), wandering through the rainforest canopy at **Otway Fly Treetop Adventures** – others are less familiar. Few know that just outside Forrest, tranquil **Lake Elizabeth** is one of the best places in Australia to spot platypuses, particularly when canoeing with a local expert. Another mysterious local creature is the fungus gnat larva (native glow-worm), which inhabits particularly cool, wet sections of the

✎ Making Waves

At the eastern edge of the Great Ocean Road lies surfing mecca **Bells Beach**. Head there early in the morning to watch pros ride its world-famous right-hand breaks, at their peak in autumn and winter. Inspired? **Go Ride a Wave** (gorideawave.com.au) runs lessons along the Great Ocean Road.

Left Great Ocean Road aerial view **Top left** Otway Fly Treetop Adventures **Top right** Koala, Great Otway National Park

rainforest. As darkness falls, rug up and take a walk along the **Maits Rest Trail** (800m) near Cape Otway or **Madsens Track Nature Walk** (1.5km) at Melba Gully (west of Lavers Hill). Eyes adjusted to the darkness, you will see them, their delicate blue-green threads glowing ethereally in the dark.

Apostles, Shipwrecks & Treasure

Rising out of savage, shipwrecking waters, the **Twelve Apostles** make for a grand finale at the western end of the Great Ocean Road. The monumental limestone stacks are especially spectacular juxtaposed against the setting sun, shortly after which little penguins begin waddling out of the ocean on their way home (bring binoculars). Further west, **Loch Ard Gorge** is where the two sole survivors of the *Loch Ard* – a British iron clipper wrecked nearby in 1878 – swam to safety. Washed-up cargo included the Loch Ard Peacock, a life-size majolica sculpture bound for Melbourne's Great Exhibition of 1880. Valued at over

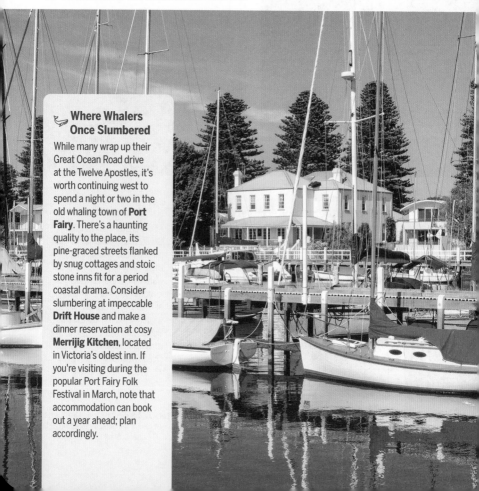

🐋 Where Whalers Once Slumbered

While many wrap up their Great Ocean Road drive at the Twelve Apostles, it's worth continuing west to spend a night or two in the old whaling town of **Port Fairy**. There's a haunting quality to the place, its pine-graced streets flanked by snug cottages and stoic stone inns fit for a period coastal drama. Consider slumbering at impeccable **Drift House** and make a dinner reservation at cosy **Merrijig Kitchen**, located in Victoria's oldest inn. If you're visiting during the popular Port Fairy Folk Festival in March, note that accommodation can book out a year ahead; plan accordingly.

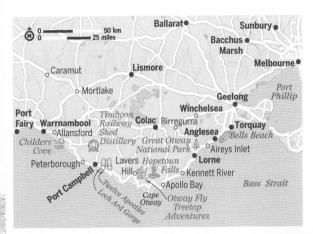

Left Moyne River, Port Fairy **Below** Childers Cove

$4 million, the exquisite Minton piece is now on display at Warrnambool's **Flagstaff Hill Maritime Museum**. Just east of Warrnambool lies **Childers Cove**, a beautiful, solitary beach that's one of the Great Ocean Road's best-kept secrets.

Savour the Region

Don't just see the Great Ocean Road; taste it. Feast on Matt Germanchis' next-level fish and chips at **Fish by Moonlite** in Anglesea and sip Ann Houlihan's native-botanicals gin at Aireys Inlet's **Great Ocean Road Gin**. Down by Apollo Bay's harbour, **Apollo Bay Fishermen's Co-op** both sells and cooks off-the-boat local fish and southern rock lobsters, caught sustainably by local skipper 'Frosty' and his crew. Inland from the Twelve Apostles, Josh Walker crafts elegant single-malt whisky at his **Timboon Railway Shed Distillery**, which also stocks local artisanal comestibles. North of the Otway Ranges, in sleepy Birregurra, you'll need to book a few months ahead for a table at Dan Hunter's internationally acclaimed farmhouse restaurant **Brae**, where extraordinary degustations might include a guided walk through the produce garden.

28 The Great OCEAN WALK

WILDLIFE | RAINFOREST | BEACHES

▬▬▬ The Great Ocean Road may be one of the world's most famous coastal drives, but that doesn't mean you need a car to enjoy its exhilarating landscapes. On the spectacular, six- to eight-day Great Ocean Walk, you can venture deep into the region's pristine rainforest, camp by wild beaches and traverse dramatic clifftops.

MARCELLA MIRIELLO/SHUTTERSTOCK ©

🗺 How to

Getting here Apollo Bay is 196km southwest of Melbourne. V-Line has a daily train-bus connection via Melbourne and Geelong.

When to go March to June and September to November are the best times weather-wise, but check school-holiday dates in June and September.

Tour operators Though many hikers complete the walk independently, tour operators can arrange guided and self-guided trips, shuttle transfers, food drops and camp set-ups. Consult www.greatoceanwalk. info or www.greatocean roadshuttle.com.au.

CASEYJADE.W/SHUTTERSTOCK ©

IAN CROCKER/SHUTTERSTOCK ©

Left Boardwalk, Great Otway National Park **Far left top** Cape Otway Lighthouse **Far left bottom** Children looking at wild echidna

The Walk

Starting in the seaside hamlet of Apollo Bay, the epic, 110km (one way) Great Ocean Walk is wondrous from the get-go. It'll have you journeying across coastal clifftops and onto the sands of rugged, remote surf beaches before leading you into beautiful rainforest. Winding through glorious Great Otway National Park, you'll pass tree ferns, grass trees and towering eucalypts before returning to the beach, punctuated by Cape Otway Lighthouse. Along the way you'll hear tales of shipwrecks, spot koalas in the trees, and feast your eyes on sublime natural attractions. The climax awaits at the finish line: there before you is the unforgettable sight of the Twelve Apostles, rising majestically from the sea.

Indigenous History

As you walk along the sands and forests of Great Otway National Park, reflect on the Gadubanud Traditional Owners who've lived on these lands for tens of thousands of years. The best place to learn about their ancient culture is at Cape Otway Lighthouse, which has guided walks, bush-tucker tours and a keeping place displaying artefacts.

Camping & Wildlife

Dedicated hiker campsites add another layer of appeal to this memorable journey. You'll encounter plenty of wildlife, from koalas at Cape Otway to eastern grey kangaroos, wallabies and echidnas. From June to August you might see migrating southern right whales off the coast.

 Perfect Pit Stops

Crayfish Bay With water under 2m deep, and protected by a reef, this is Australia's number-one beach. Even on a 'crowded' day there are never more than six people here.

Ryan's Den Lights. Camera. Action. Sit and wait while you enjoy the view, keeping your camera on standby for that ultimate shot.

Melanesia Beach Hike to the Great Ocean Walk's strangest beach to see 'cannonballs' embedded in the rockfall. Pack a picnic and take a friend to enjoy its magic.

 ■ **Recommended by Mark Brack,** local Otway expert and experienced tour guide www.greatoceanwalk.info/mark-brack-shipwreck-tours

THE GIPPSLAND COAST

COAST | WILDERNESS | FOOD

THE GIPPSLAND COAST
Trip Builder

Goulburn

New South Wales

⊗ Canberra

Australian Capital Territory (ACT)

Stretching out across Victoria's far east is this pristine expanse of coastal wilderness that mixes remote beaches with outdoor adventure and artisanal produce. In between exploring national parks, you'll visit laid-back towns that entice with breweries, distilleries and wineries, among other epicurean temptations.

Sit back and enjoy life on a houseboat in **Mallacoota** (p171)
🚗 4hrs from Lakes Entrance

Spot koalas while strolling **Raymond Island** (p171)
🚗 40mins from Bairnsdale

Drop by for street food and inventive craft beers at **Sailors Grave Brewing** (p169)
🚗 1¼hrs from Lakes Entrance

Cann River   Genoa

Get on your bike to tackle a leg of the **Great Southern Rail Trail** (p171)
🚗 45mins from Wilsons Promontory

Bairnsdale

Paynesville

🍺 **Orbost**

Go for a paddle to explore the beautiful waters of **Lakes Entrance** (p171)
🚗 1hr from Bairnsdale

Warragul **Moe** **Sale**
Traralgon

Bass Strait

Foster 🚲**Yarram**

Inverloch

Hike out to spend a night in 19th-century **Wilsons Promontory Lighthouse** (p175)
🚶 2 days from Tidal River

Jet out to see the mysterious **Skull Rock** (p173)
🚗 3hrs from Melbourne

LKONYA/SHUTTERSTOCK ©

N   0 _____ 50 km
     0 _____ 25 miles

Practicalities

ARRIVING

Melbourne Airport From here it's a 1½-hour drive to South Gippsland's coast.

Southern Cross Station Has buses to South Gippsland and a train to Bairnsdale Station for bus connections throughout East Gippsland.

FIND YOUR WAY

Tourist info centres in Gippsland's coastal towns have maps, brochures and helpful staff (visitgippsland.com.au).

MONEY

Free campsites are located along the dunes of Ninety Mile Beach, the perfect spot to reel in your own dinner.

WHERE TO STAY

Location	Atmosphere
Tidal River	The visitor hub for Wilsons Promontory National Park has an excellent mix of safari tents, cabins & campsites.
Lakes Entrance	This tourist town is filled with family-friendly accommodation.
Mallacoota	A super-chilled, old-school coastal destination that's all about relaxed caravan parks, waterfront camping and houseboats.

EATING & DRINKING

If you like to keep things local, sustainable, organic, experimental, rustic, scenic and, above all, delicious, then you've definitely come to the right place. With its huge coastline of fresh seafood and rolling green dairy farms, Gippsland offers gourmet produce that'll be the highlight of your visit.

Best winery
Lightfoot Wines (p169; pictured top)

Must-try seafood
Sardine (p169; pictured bottom)

GETTING AROUND

Car Hiring a car is by far the best way to explore the region, and it's the only way to access Wilsons Prom.

Bus Services run to most townships throughout the region, but not the national parks.

Train Services run from Spencer Street Station to Bairnsdale Station, from where buses run to East Gippsland destinations.

JAN–MAR Peak season, with perfect beach weather

APR–JUN Mixed bag weatherwise, but ideal for hikes and camping

JUL–SEP Cold, blustery conditions add to the coastal romance

OCT–DEC Delightful weather and fewer visitors

29 Gippsland for **EPICURES**

FOOD | DRINK | LOCAL

In recent years Gippsland has attracted acclaimed chefs, respected winemakers and artisanal producers, all here to capitalise on the region's gourmet bounty. Their work is showcased across cellar doors, high-end restaurants and local farmers markets. From seafood and speciality cheeses to breweries and distilleries, there are plenty of ways to indulge along Gippsland's food-and-wine trail.

DESTINATION GIPPSLAND ©

🗺 How to

Getting here & around
Some attractions can be reached by public transport, but for the most part a car is necessary. Otherwise, join a tour with Gippsland Food Adventures (gippsland foodadventures.com.au).

When to go Year-round; reservations are required during peak periods.

Wineries One of Australia's up-and-coming wine destinations, the area has soil ripe for viticulture. Pinot noir and chardonnay are the region's specialities; see winegippsland.com.

HOGGET ©

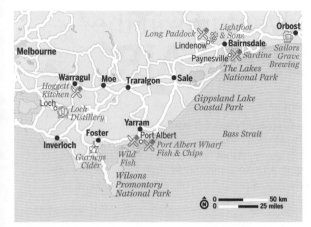

Far left top Lightfoot Wines **Far left bottom** Charcuterie, Hogget Kitchen

Seafood

Unpretentious fine-dining restaurant **Sardine** in Paynesville is one of the best places to sample delicious seafood, serving sublime contemporary and seasonal dishes. You won't get classic fish and chips any fresher than at **Port Albert Wharf Fish & Chips**. Here it's all straight off the boat, as it is next door at the sit-down Mod Oz restaurant **Wild Fish**.

Farm Produce

Gippsland is famous for its rolling green paddocks, so dairy and farm produce is another reason to visit. **Hogget Kitchen** in Warragul is well worth the inland detour for its award-winning menu of paddock-to-plate dishes and estate-grown wines. **Long Paddock** in Lindenow is run by a husband-wife team with a wealth of experience in some of the world's finest restaurants.

Cellar Doors

Gippsland boasts an array of top-shelf booze produced by talented locals. For a fine single malt look no further than **Loch Distillery**, which also makes artisanal gins and ales. **Sailors Grave Brewing** in Orbost is one of Australia's most respected microbreweries, producing experimental beers using local, seasonal ingredients. Fans of traditional cider should stop by **Gurneys Cider** just outside Wilsons Prom, where an expat family of Brits makes the real thing. And for wonderful cool-climate maritime wines, **Lightfoot Wines** delivers the goods with award-winning pinot noir and chardonnay.

Sips, Treats & Eats

Gurneys Cider Stunning views of Wilsons Prom and some of the best ciders in Australia.

Lightfoot Wines Has an amazing cellar door and makes some of our favourite local wines.

Gippsland Jersey After a lot of road testing we can confirm the butter here is the best. We eat it like cheese on fresh baguettes from **Seasalt Sourdough Bakery**.

East Gippsland Coffee Roasters A must-stop if you're passing through, this hole-in-the-wall place is just up the street from our brewery.

Marlo Hotel We always take visitors here. Overlooking the mouth of the Snowy, it's excellent for a fresh Sou'East Draught on the deck.

■ Recommended by Gab and Chris Moore, *Sailors Grave Brewing, Orbost* @sailorsgravebrewing

30 Adventures in the OPEN AIR

PADDLING | CYCLING | DIVING

████ Immerse yourself in Gippsland's natural beauty as you hike, cycle or stand-up paddleboard (SUP) along its stunning landscapes. Most visitors are here to get out on the water: the sparkling lakes and alluring beaches are perfect for swimming, surfing, kayaking and snorkelling. Fishing is the other big lure, providing the perfect way to unwind from the stresses of modern life.

ANDREW BAIN/ALAMY STOCK PHOTO ©

🗺 How to

Getting here & around
Lakes Entrance can be reached by train-bus connection from Melbourne via Bairnsdale Station. From Lakes Entrance, local buses go further afield, including to Mallacoota.

When to go The shoulder seasons (March to June and September to November) bring lovely weather and fewer crowds.

Surf's up! From monster breaks to learner waves, Gippsland is blessed with surf spots to suit all levels. Newbies can get in touch with Surf Shack (surfshack.com.au).

AULD/DIST/GETTY IMAGES ©

Far left top Bass Coast Rail Trail **Far left bottom** Young fisher, Mallacoota

THE GIPPSLAND COAST EXPERIENCES

Heli-SUP

A collaboration by **Lakes Entrance Helicopters** and **Venture Out**, these exhilarating trips take you up in a chopper for an unforgettable coastal flight before landing on Ninety Mile Beach, from where you return via guided SUP tour along the sparkling Gippsland Lakes. Helicopters depart from Lakes Entrance.

Diving & Snorkelling

An underwater world awaits along the Gippsland coast, with reefs teeming with marine life. **Cross Diving** runs diving and snorkelling trips to Bunurong Marine National Park and Cape Conran, where you'll encounter a rich diversity of fish, weedy sea dragons, kelp forests and shipwrecks. Further east, far-flung Gabo Island is another magical spot.

Houseboats

Fishing, swimming, reading, drinking – life doesn't get much more relaxed than a few days spent lazing on a houseboat. In East Gippsland, **Mallacoota Wilderness Houseboats** kits out boats with all the mod cons, ensuring you enjoy nature in style.

Cycling

With a mix of bike paths, rail trails and MTB parks, coastal Gippsland is a wonderful destination to explore on two wheels. A highlight is the **Great Southern Rail Trail**: pedal along a 72km path that follows the old train line past some of Gippsland's less-visited coastal hamlets and country towns. The shorter **Bass Coast Rail Trail** (21km) is another great option for exploring South Gippsland's beaches and countryside.

East Gippsland Rambles

Ninety Mile Beach If you like long walks on the beach you're gonna love this one – all 90 miles of it! Stretching from Port Welshpool to Lakes Entrance, this wild and remote stretch of surf beach can be tackled as individual walks.

Raymond Island Koala Walk A memorable 3km walk loops around tiny Raymond Island (koala islandfoundation.com.au), allowing you glimpses of its koala population, along with echidnas, kangaroos, wombats and plenty of birds.

Lakes Entrance A stunning 5km coastal trail rewards with dramatic views over the Entrance, where the Gippsland Lakes empty into the ocean.

31

Wilsons Prom
WONDERS

WALKS | WILDERNESS | BEACHES

▬▬▬ Turquoise waters and bone-white sands meet pristine bushland at Wilsons Promontory (affectionately known in Victoria as 'the Prom'). A very popular place for hiking and camping, this is one of Australia's most spectacular swathes of coastal wilderness.

WILSONS PROMONTORY CRUISES ©

🗺 How to

Getting here & around
Tidal River is 224km southeast of Melbourne. You'll need your own vehicle, as there's no public transport. Otherwise, Hike & Seek (hikeandseek.com.au) runs day tours.

When to go August to November is ideal, with spring wildflowers, whale watching, temperate weather and lighter crowds.

Wildlife From inquisitive wombats at your campsite to kangaroos and emus along the **Prom Wildlife Walk** (2.3km return), this is a destination rich in native fauna.

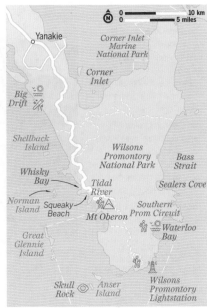

Skull Rock

Emerging from the sea like a movie villain's lair is the remote and enigmatic island known as Skull Rock. Until recently the monolith was off limits to tourists, but thanks to **Wilsons Promontory Cruises** you can now get up close to its 130m-wide cave. Getting here is half the fun: cool amphibious boats pick you up from the sands of Norman Beach for a memorable 2½-hour tour of the Prom's unique coastal wilderness. This is Victoria's largest marine protected area, so you'll pass islands home to seals, penguins and mutton birds. Keep an eye out for bottlenose dolphins and, from May to October, southern right whales.

Southern Prom Circuit

One of the best ways to experience the Prom is to strap on your boots and set out on a long walk through part of its vast wilderness. Hikes last anywhere from 30 minutes to a week, and there are all kinds of trails depending on your time and energy. Stretching

Left Bottlenose dolphin
Above left Skull Rock

over 36km, the Southern Prom Circuit is the park's signature trek, a three-day, two-night camping adventure showcasing the Prom's stunning biodiversity. Wending through warm temperate rainforest, the route takes in eucalypt-scented forests, verdant fern gullies and mountaintop lookouts before concluding at blissful white-sand beaches where you can camp overlooking calm azure waters.

Big Drift

Though there's no shortage of golden beaches across Wilsons Prom, there's nothing else quite as monumental as the sands found at the Big Drift. These spectacular inland dunes rise from the encroaching woodland in a surreal and unexpected sight: it feels as though you've landed on another planet as you wander across the evocative landscape

🚶 Best Prom Hikes

Sealers Cove Along the walk you'll see multiple forest types and ecosystems, and you'll get to visit Sealers Cove (one of Australia's best beaches!). Approximately five hours return.

Mt Oberon Lookout This is an unmissable, world-class panorama overlooking Wilsons Prom. The best time to visit is at sunset. Approximately 2½ hours return.

Beach trifecta Starting at Tidal River campground, you can walk to Squeaky Beach, Picnic Bay and Whisky Bay via coastal walking tracks and beaches. Approximately three hours return, but you'll want to spend longer on the beach!

■ **Recommended by Bill Gurnett,** *former Parks Victoria ranger and current co-owner of Gurneys Cider* @gurneyscidery

🔦 Wilsons Prom Lightstation

You can sleep in a 19th-century cottage at mainland Australia's most southerly lighthouse. Mind you, you'll earn your rest: to get here you must walk 20km (one way) through the Prom's beautiful hinterland. Climb to the top of the windswept beacon for views over Bass Strait.

admiring views over the expansive Vereker Range bushland and the distant ocean. For the best photos, come at sunrise or sunset, when the sands glow rose gold. If you're into stargazing, come back at night to witness a spectacular galactic light show. Sandboarding is also a thing here, so if you've got an old boogie board, bring it along to surf the Big Drift's sandy swells.

Walks from Tidal River

If you're not sold on a multiday wilderness hike, you'll be relieved to hear that many of the Prom's iconic attractions are only a short stroll from the park's headquarters at Tidal River. If you have time for just one walk, make it the trip up **Mt Oberon**. At the summit you'll be treated to all-encompassing, life-affirming vistas across the entire national park. A beach walk is also a good choice. The most well known of these is the walk to the aptly named **Squeaky Beach**, which makes sounds like a dog toy as you stroll across its powdery quartz sands. Equally spectacular is nearby **Whisky Bay**, with its chalky white sands, sparkling aquamarine waters and photogenic lichen-splattered boulders.

Left Hiker, Wilsons Promontory
Above top Squeaky Beach **Above**
Blotched blue-tongued lizard, Wilsons Promontory National Park

Listings

BEST OF THE REST

National Parks

Croajingolong National Park

One of Australia's finest swathes of coastal wilderness, this Unesco Biosphere Reserve features untouched beaches, towering dunes, great fishing and oceanfront camping. The region was badly hit by the 2020 bushfires, so check conditions ahead of your visit.

Cape Conran Coastal Park

This protected area in East Gippsland is perfect for blissful summers of swimming, surfing, fishing, camping, reading and long walks along its beautiful beach.

The Lakes National Park

Mixing Ninety Mile Beach with the serene Gippsland Lakes is this biodiverse marine park that's all about unwinding by the water.

Fresh Local Food

Farmers Markets

From Koonwarra and Korumburra to Meeniyan and Mirboo North, Gippsland is known for its farmers markets, which take place across its rural townships on a rotating schedule.

Prom Country Cheese

When it comes to Gippsland produce, dairy is king – cheese especially! Drop by this farmhouse to taste an array of gourmet sheep's- and cow's-milk cheeses.

Lakes Entrance Fishermen's Co-op

While many visitors come to Gippsland to reel in their own dinner, don't despair if you didn't bring your fishing gear. Located on Bullock Island, the Lakes Entrance co-op is a popular spot to stock up on some of the local catch to cook up back home.

Prom Coast Ice Cream

With all that dairy it'd be a shame if you couldn't get local ice cream. Fortunately, Prom Coast whips the likes of salted-caramel ripple and various fruit sorbets, all made using Gippsland cream.

Coastal Pubs

Kilcunda Ocean View Hotel $$

The well-loved 'Killy' enjoys 180-degree ocean views. A popular stop for a beer and a feed on the journey from Melbourne to Gippsland, it's also accessible along the Bass Coast Rail Trail.

Metung Hotel $$

Overlooking the yacht-filled waters of the Gippsland Lakes, this Metung institution has been drawing tourists and locals alike for over 100 years for pub meals and drinks with a view.

Waterwheel Beach Tavern $$

Offering a low-key alternative to its more famous neighbour Lakes Entrance, Lake Tyers has a ripper coastal pub across from Ninety Mile Beach. Come for fresh fish and chips, and local craft beers.

Croajingolong National Park

Marlo Hotel $$

Sitting at the confluence of the Snowy River and the ocean, this East Gippy fave lures in farmers, fishers and just about everyone else for cold drinks, bistro meals and the relaxed atmosphere on its deck.

LakeView Bar & Bistro $$

In Loch Spot, the secluded LakeView sits right on the lakeshore. Life doesn't get more relaxed than sitting here with a cold drink in hand.

Fish Creek Hotel $$

Gateway pub to Wilsons Prom, this art deco hotel has long served as the pride of Fish Creek, offering a quality Gippsland wine and beer menu to go with all the pub-grub classics.

Archies Creek Hotel $$

A 10-minute drive from the beach, the Archies Creek Hotel offers a rock 'n' vibe, with live gigs to go with a quality menu of local produce.

🏮 Lighthouses

Point Hicks Lighthouse

Hidden away in remote East Gippsland's Croajingolong National Park is this secluded lighthouse built in the 1880s. Take the 162 steps to the top for dramatic views and perhaps even spend a night in its lighthouse keeper's cottage.

Gabo Island Lighthouse

Accessible only by boat or chartered flight, Gabo Island is home to Australia's second-tallest lighthouse (47m). You can spend the night in its assistant lighthouse keeper's cottage, dating to 1862, alongside your neighbours: penguins and seals.

Cape Liptrap Lighthouse

Guarding South Gippsland's rocky coastline is Cape Liptrap's octagonal 1950s lighthouse, reached via a clifftop trail that offers astounding coastal vistas.

Point Hicks Lighthouse

◎ Ancient Sights

Bataluk Cultural Trail

Running from Sale to Cape Conran, this road trip takes in Aboriginal cultural sites across East Gippsland. Stops include sacred caves, coastal middens, hunting areas and wooded wetlands (batalukculturaltrail.com.au).

Krowathunkooloong Keeping Place

Located in Bairnsdale, the Krowathunkooloong Keeping Place (gegac.org.au/keepingplace) is a must-see for those who want to learn about Aboriginal history and culture. The focus is on the Gunaikurnai people, the Traditional Owners of the East Gippsland area.

East Cape Boardwalk

A featured stop along the Bataluk Cultural Trail, this coastal boardwalk in Cape Conran tells the story of the Gunaikurnai people who came to Salmon Rock to feast on seafood.

Dinosaur Traces

Predating humans by some 130 million years, South Gippsland's dinosaurs roamed across what is now Inverloch's Bunurong Marine Park. Many fossils have been found in the region, and remarkably you can even observe a dinosaur footprint (sgcs.org.au/dinosaurs.php), embedded in the rock pools and visible only at low tide.

THE GIPPSLAND COAST REVIEWS

BRISBANE & SOUTHEAST QUEENSLAND

WILDLIFE | BEER | BEACHES

Experience Brisbane & Southeast Queensland online

BRISBANE & SOUTHEAST QUEENSLAND
Trip Builder

Just call it 300 days of summer. That's how many days of annual sunshine you can expect in southeast Queensland (SEQ), which stretches from the NSW border through the Gold Coast's theme parks to the Sunshine Coast's surf breaks and inland to wild rainforest.

Camp beside sublime blue swimming holes in **Conondale National Park** (p199)
🚗 *2hrs from the Sunshine Coast*

Conondale National Park   Maleny

Woodford

Get up early to spot platypuses in **Maleny's Obi Obi Creek** (p202)
🚗 *45mins from the Sunshine Coast*

Lake Wivenhoe

● **Gatton**

Toowoomba

● **Ipswich**

Sample fresh camel's milk in the **Scenic Rim Region** (p186)
🚗 *1½hrs from Brisbane*

QUEENSLAND

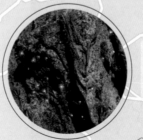

Find rare glow-worms lighting up the night in **Springbrook National Park** (p189)
🚗 *45mins from the Gold Coast*

NEW SOUTH WALES

Noosa
Heads

Maroochydore

Chug a beer or five on a
Sunshine Coast craft-
brewery tour (p190)
🚗 1½hrs from Brisbane

Caloundra

*Bribie
Island*

*Moreton
Island*

*Moreton
Bay*

*South
Pacific
Ocean*

BRISBANE

Learn to identify bush tucker
on **Stradbroke Island** with a
Quandamooka guide (p192)
⛴ 30mins from Brisbane

*North
Stradbroke
Island*

*South
Stradbroke
Island*

Indulge at award-winning
restaurants on the **Gold
Coast** (p184)
🚗 1hr from Brisbane

Southport

Beaudesert

Surfers Paradise

Burleigh
Heads

*Springbrook
National
Park*

Coolangatta

*Lamington
National
Park*

**Explore bookable
experiences in
Brisbane & Southeast
Queensland online**

Practicalities

CHAMELEONSEYE/SHUTTERSTOCK ©

ARRIVING

Gold Coast Airport Catch a flight direct from major Australian cities to this regional airport.

Brisbane International Airport Halfway between the Gold and Sunshine Coasts, this is the largest, busiest and most centrally located airport in the region. It's about a 20-minute drive from the airport to the city.

Sunshine Coast Airport In Marcoola, this small airport has daily flights to Adelaide, Melbourne, Sydney, Cairns and Canberra.

HOW MUCH FOR A

Craft-beer tasting flight $15

1hr SUP paddle-board rental $25

Hinterland cottage stay $175

GETTING AROUND

Bus, ferry & train TransLink covers the entire SEQ region, with services extending from Coolangatta in the south to Noosa Heads in the north. A commuter train runs from Varsity Lakes to Cooroy. Purchase a Go card from stations or retailers for discounted fares.

Car While most of the Gold Coast, Brisbane and destinations along the Bruce Hwy are well serviced by public transport, it can be time-consuming and difficult to access the Sunshine Coast coastline or hinterland this way. For flexibility, rent a car.

Island ferry SeaLink and Stradbroke Flyer car and passenger ferries go to Stradbroke Island. For Moreton Island, Micat operates on a demand-based timetable.

WHEN TO GO

JAN–MAR
Hot, humid and rainy, with temperatures that climb above 25°C

APR–JUN
Clear skies and pleasant, mild weather

JUL–SEP
Mild near the coast; chilly mornings and nights in the hinterlands

OCT–DEC
Blooming jacarandas herald spring; warm, sunny days

EATING & DRINKING

Like the rest of Australia's East Coast, SEQ is known for its seafood, including Moreton Bay bugs (pictured right) . Named after the bay near Brisbane, they're not insects but rather a lobster-like crustacean.

On menus at many fine-dining restaurants you may see bush-tucker (native food) ingredients. These indigenous animals, insects and plants were traditionally used as meals or medicine by Aboriginal peoples.

Feeling thirsty? Choose from dozens of craft brewers and distillers.

Best craft beer	Must-try bush honey
Brouhaha Brewery (p191)	Yura Tours on Stradbroke Island (p194)

CONNECT & FIND YOUR WAY

Wi-fi Few cafes offer free wi-fi; try a library or one of the networks on the Gold and Sunshine Coasts and in Brisbane.

Navigation The M1 highway runs along the entirety of the coast but can slow to a snail's pace during peak hour. The inland routes are less direct, but less hectic and considerably more scenic.

DISCOUNTS

The official regional tourism organisations – visitbrisbane. com.au, visitsunshinecoast. com and destinationgoldcoast. com – feature discount codes and exclusive deals on accommodation and activities.

WHERE TO STAY

Brisbane has accommodation options for all budgets and tastes. Elsewhere, the further you are from the coastline, the more limited your choices become.

Location	Atmosphere
Surfers Paradise, Broadbeach, Miami & Main Beach	Motels, apartments, midrange hotels and luxury accommodation, all within easy walking distance of the beach.
Gold Coast Hinterland	Camping, glamping and luxury health retreats surrounded by native bush.
Brisbane CBD, South Bank, West End & Fortitude Valley	Four- and five-star hotels in the centre of the action.
Sunshine Coast	Primarily tourist apartments and private rentals, with views of the coastline.
Montville & Maleny	B&Bs, cottages and boutique family-owned inns high in the hinterland.

MONEY

Passion fruit, pineapples, avocados: you name it and you'll probably find it being sold roadside. Most farmgate stalls are unstaffed and cash only, operating on the honour system; have gold ($1 and $2) coins handy.

BRISBANE & SOUTHEAST QUEENSLAND FIND YOUR FEET

32 Glitz, Glamour & **GLUTTONY**

CAFES | COCKTAILS | DINING

▬▬▬ Not long ago, food on the Gold Coast was synonymous with greasy takeaway designed to sop up hangovers. But over the last decade the place has been transformed into a five-star foodie destination, with top chefs from Sydney and Melbourne decamping to the stretch between Broadbeach and Burleigh. Family-friendly beachside venues, chic cafes and glitzy cocktail bars are all on offer.

THE MILKMAN'S DAUGHTER @THEMILKMANSDAUGHTER_GC ©

🗺 **How to**

When to go Cafe kitchens close as early as 2pm. Cocktails and bar snacks can be found around the clock; dinner service starts around 6pm.

What's in a hat? Awarded annually by the *Australian Good Food Guide*, 'hats' are the country's most prestigious culinary awards.

Pace yourself Free-flowing drinks aren't restricted to weekends: bottomless brunches can be found up and down the coast on any day of the week.

MAYA SCHOLZ/PADDOCK BAKERY ©

Broadbeach o

Elk Espresso

Lupo

Milkman's
Daughter

Mermaid Beach o

Nobby Beach

Miami

Robina

Paddock Bakery

Coral
Sea

Burleigh Heads o

Restaurant Labart

Burleigh
Pavilion

West
Burleigh

Pasture & Co.
(7km)

Palm Beach

Far left top Vegetarian dishes,
Milkman's Daughter **Far left
bottom** Crème brûlée doughnut,
Paddock Bakery

Early-morning indulgence Arrive early to score a seat in
the garden at **Paddock Bakery** in Burleigh Heads, the most
awarded cafe on the coast. Inside, watch pastry chefs at work
whipping up Nutella cruffins or Paddock's trademark crème
brûlée doughnuts. For a boozier brunch, there's **Elk Espresso**
in Broadbeach, where bottomless mimosas are served daily
from 10am to 2pm.

Afternoon tipple The mandate is endless summer at casual,
beachside **Burleigh Pavilion**. Jugs of Pimm's, freshly shucked
oysters and resident DJs are ensuring it meets its goal. To
guarantee a seat with ocean views, make a reservation at the
Tropic, the Pavilion's full-service establishment.

Get glammed up The Gold Coast has more than a dozen
hatted restaurants, including **Restaurant Labart** in Burleigh
Heads. The menu changes regularly, but anticipate dishes
such as Moreton Bay bugs in shellfish broth, or candy melon
and Queensland scallops served with kumquat. Vegetarian
options are available, and bookings are required.

After the after-party Although fresh seafood tends to be
the name of the Gold Coast game, the local produce is worth
celebrating, too. Try the sweet mango tacos at the **Milkman's
Daughter** in Mermaid Waters, or head to **Pasture & Co.** in
Currumbin Village: surrounded by 100-year-old fig trees, the
cafe caters to every dietary need imaginable, including paleo,
vegan, nut-free and gluten-free.

From Dawn to Dessert

For breakfast or brunch:
Highline, Palm Beach.
Owner Tim Casagrande
has worked with key Aus-
tralian roasters. His team
makes the best coffee and
their brekkie dishes are
executed perfectly.

For afternoon drinks:
Rosella's Bar, Burleigh
Heads. Enjoy innovative
cocktails – like the
Margot-rita Robbie, made
with wattle blossom and
roasted kelp – and a fun
environment.

For dinner: Lupo,
Mermaid Beach. The
love that goes into this
family-owned restaurant is
clear from a mile away. The
Mediterranean and Italian
flavours are spot on.

For dessert: Scoop Gelati,
Burleigh Heads. It always
has interesting flavour
combinations, such as
mango macadamia.

■ Tips by Alex
Munoz Labart,
*chef and owner
of Restaurant
Labart and Paloma Wine Bar*
@restaurantlabart

BRISBANE & SOUTHEAST QUEENSLAND EXPERIENCES

The Camel Connection

SOUTHEAST QUEENSLAND'S CAMEL DAIRIES REVEAL AN UNTOLD HISTORY

There will never be an animal more synonymous with Australia than the kangaroo, more beloved than the koala or more feared than the crocodile. Yet camels – despite not being an indigenous species – have managed to cement their place in the country's iconography.

CHERYL BRONSON/GETTY IMAGES ©

Camels in Australian Culture

At the turn of the 20th century, camels were used by police officers to patrol rural areas, in Australia's very own version of the mounted police. In 1977 camels were the pack-animal companions to adventurer Robyn Davidson when she spent nine months trekking from Alice Springs to the Western Australian coast (a journey she wrote about in her 1980 book *Tracks,* the basis of the 2013 movie of the same name). Every year thousands of people descend upon Yulara in the Northern Territory to watch jockeys racing astride the ungulates, and as a tourist you can ride around Uluru on one.

Camel Milk

In southeast Queensland, entrepreneurial farmers are milking the invasive species for what they're worth – literally.

Some of the biggest camel dairies in the world are located just outside Brisbane, selling a product that's gaining superfood status. Camel milk is a low-lactose option that's touted as a cure for everything from eczema to diabetes. It's also arguably a more ethical animal milk. Unlike a dairy cow – which must be separated from her calf when it's born in order to give milk for just six to nine months – a camel can share her milk with the farmer and her calf for up to 18 months. Domesticating and milking the feral animals also saves them from being culled. With an estimated two million camels roaming freely through the outback, Australia is said to have the largest camel herd in the world.

But a visit to one of SEQ's camel dairies isn't just a chance to learn about the burgeoning industry – it's also an opportunity to understand a piece of Australian history that could otherwise easily be missed.

Left Camel calf **Middle** Camel, wombat and kangaroo warning sign **Right** Riding camels on the beach

Cameleers

The one-humped dromedaries were introduced to Australia in the 1840s. Identified for their suitability for the outback landscape, they were imported en masse, and became the primary means for transporting goods through the centre of the country. They didn't come along, though – they were accompanied by camel drivers from what are now Afghanistan, Pakistan and India.

> With an estimated two million camels roaming freely through the outback, Australia is said to have the largest camel herd in the world.

These cameleers and their steeds played a critical role in opening up the interior of Australia. In addition to hauling supplies, they helped build railways and the Australian Overland Telegraph Line between Adelaide and Darwin. But by the 1930s the introduction of the motor vehicle had rendered their services obsolete. Faced with hostility – including discriminatory government policies that prevented them from obtaining citizenship – many cameleers were forced to pack up and return home.

Yet you can still see traces of their impact on Australia. In Brisbane's Holland Park, for example, you'll find the site of Queensland's first formal mosque. Dating back to the 1880s, it's also home to Queensland's Muslim Museum, where you can learn about the cameleers' early contributions to the country. But one of the biggest marks they left on the landscape is the intelligent and resilient animals they had to leave behind.

⌂ Camel Cuddles

In the Scenic Rim Region, just 65km southwest of Brisbane, **Summer Land Camels** is the largest commercial camel dairy outside the Middle East, and the third largest of its kind in the world. At its cafe you can look out onto the paddocks as you sample camel cheese, camel gelato or a latte made with camel milk, and slather your hands with camel-milk beauty products. Family-friendly farm tours and camel rides are also available.

The award-winning **QCamel Milk Dairy** in the Glass House Mountains offers a similar experience, with 'camel cuddles' every first and third Saturday of the month. Bookings are essential.

33 Rainforest **RETREAT**

BUSHWALKING | GLOW-WORMS | SPAS

With its casinos, nightclubs and theme parks, the Gold Coast is renowned for being a little bit extra. But go inland and you'll find excess of an entirely different sort. With a geological history dating back more than 225 million years, the Gold Coast hinterland is home to around 500 waterfalls, 390 wildlife species and hundreds of kilometres of bushwalking tracks.

JESSICA WYNNE LOCKHART ©

🗺 **How to**

Getting here Budget ample time. The road to Lamington National Park is single lane at times, with hairpin turns and monster potholes. Southern Cross Tours offers day trips.

When to go At an elevation of 1000m, the hinterland is 5°C to 8°C cooler than the coast. For gushing waterfalls, visit between November and March.

What to pack Bring long pants to ward off leeches, and a torch (flashlight) for nocturnal wildlife spotting.

JESSICA WYNNE LOCKHART ©

Far left top O'Reilly's Rainforest Retreat **Far left bottom** Gwinganna Lifestyle Retreat

Bushwalking Although Tamborine Mountain has long been the go-to, many prefer the tranquillity of Springbrook and Lamington National Parks.

There are really only two spots to stay in Lamington: **Binna Burra Lodge** on the eastern side and **O'Reilly's Rainforest Retreat** in the western Green Mountains section. Both offer glamping tents and lodge rooms, as well as guided tours and direct trail access. The 21.4km Border Track – part of the longer Gold Coast Hinterland Great Walk – connects the two, with shuttles making it possible to walk one way. However, there are trails for all skill levels, such as the 90-minute walk to 80m Morans Falls – listen for the mewling call of green catbirds and look for golden regent bowerbirds.

With limited accommodation, Springbrook is better tackled on a day trip, although spending the night affords you the opportunity to see pademelons, which emerge at dusk, and rare glow-worms. Both parks have few amenities, so fuel up before you leave.

Spas You're in Australia's spa capital, with some of the most luxurious hidden in the hinterland. **Gwinganna Lifestyle Retreat** in Tallebudgera Valley is a celebrity favourite; its award-winning spa is open only to guests. The same goes for treatments at the five-star **Eden Health Retreat** in Currumbin Valley. For day treatments, try the **Bathhouse at Ground Currumbin**, a newer complex with massages and cedar hot tubs.

☆ Glow Bright

Glow-worms – the larvae of *Arachnocampa* fungus gnats, and typically found in damp cave environments – are renowned for producing a blue-green bioluminescence, and this is one of the only places in the world to see it.

Australia's largest colony is under Springbrook National Park's Natural Bridge. In Lamington National Park, O'Reilly's Rainforest Retreat offers a glow-worm tour. If you're not a night owl, visit Tamborine Mountain's purpose-built caves during the day.

Fun/gross fact: it's the glow-worms' excrement that glows – but that doesn't make this experience any less ethereal. For the best viewing, avoid the use of flashlights and keep noise low.

Cool Drops for
HOT DAYS

BEER | FOOD | MUSIC

Holding the title of Australia's Craft-Beer Capital, the Sunshine Coast claims the most craft breweries per capita. The region's 21 labels (and counting) are known for their award-winning beers, busy gastropubs and live-music events. Here are five taprooms to tap into.

RILEY JUDD ©

🍺 Bold Brews

Heads of Noosa Summer Dusk Lager A roast malt character adds complexity without compromising on drinkability.

Moffat Beach Brewing Trilogy Best Coast IPA This IPA belts out pine and citrus notes. Bold, bitter and delicious.

10 Toes Vanilla Porter Velvety and smooth, but not too sweet.

🗺 Trip Notes

Getting around If you plan to visit more than one brewery – or sample more than one beer – sign up for a tour with Sunshine Coast Craft Beer Tours.

Events The Sunshine Coast Craft Beer & Cider Festival and the Hinterland Craft Beer Festival are both hosted annually.

Bring an Esky Many seasonal beers are only available direct from the breweries. Arrive prepared to take home a growler, or forever live with regret.

■ Tips by **Matt Jancauskas,** *CEO of Brouhaha Brewery* @mattbrouhaha

Cooroy

05 Although it has experimental and sessionable beers on tap, Cooroy's **Copperhead Restaurant Brewery** is just as well known for its kitchen, with offerings such as prawn and sand-crab cannelloni. Bookings recommended.

04 With food trucks, live music and even a petting zoo, **Terella Brewery** in North Arm is made for Sunday sessions. Pack a picnic rug and settle in on the large grassy area.

Eumundi

Coolum Beach

Yandina

Maroochy River

02 The name says it all: Warana's **Your Mates** is a meeting spot (complete with playground) for friends and families. Try the easy-drinking Larry Pale Ale, which ticks all the boxes on a hot day.

Bli Bli

Nambour

Woombye

Maroochydore

South Pacific Ocean

Palmwoods

Buderim

Mooloolaba

Montville

Kawana Waters

Lake Baroon

Maleny

Mooloolah River

Mooloolah

Moffat Beach Brewing Co. Production House

03 **Brouhaha**, which champions the hinterland's producers, is worth the side trip to Maleny. Don't miss the not-too-sweet Strawberry Rhubarb Sour, made with local strawberries and Maleny Dairies' yoghurt.

Landsborough

Caloundra

01 **Moffat Beach Brewing Co.** is the expert in classic pale ales. The original beachside location (pictured far left) has the ocean views, while its production outpost hosts music and comedy events.

Beerwah

Glass House Mountains

35 Escape to a Sand
ISLAND

BUSH TUCKER | WHALES | CULTURE

▬▬▬ Fondly known as 'Straddie', North Stradbroke Island (Minjerribah) is the world's second-largest sand island. Swim in freshwater lakes, stroll along empty beaches, watch humpback whales from the shore, and immerse yourself in Indigenous culture – it's all here, just 45km from Brisbane's CBD.

DARKBLUESHUTTER/SHUTTERSTOCK ©

🗺 How to

Getting here Ferries leave from Cleveland and arrive in Dunwich, with plans under way for a direct ferry from Brisbane's Howard Smith Wharves.

When to go Whale season runs from May to November.

Getting around A car is handy but not absolutely necessary. A cash-only bus runs from Dunwich to Myora, Amity Point and Point Lookout, and tour operators pick guests up from the ferry terminal. Scooter and bicycle rentals are available.

YURA TOURS ©

Take It Slow

Straddie is southeast Queensland's answer to K'gari (Fraser Island), except it's arguably more accessible (you don't need a 4WD), making it possible to experience on a day trip. But if your schedule allows, don't rush your visit – this is the kind of place where time slows and folds in on itself in the best possible way.

Quandamooka Country

The Quandamooka (people of the bay) – including the Nughi, Nunukul and Gorenpul – have continuously occupied Minjerribah and neighbouring Mulgumpin (Moreton Island) for tens of thousands of years. A visit to Straddie is an opportunity to learn about their history, including at the **Myora Mission Site**. Now a place for quiet contemplation, it's also where

LOKU/SHUTTERSTOCK ©

✅ Ask an Elder

The North Stradbroke Island Aboriginal and Islander Housing Co-Operative is a 10-minute walk from the ferry terminal in Dunwich. Drop in to meet some of the Elders, and see the display of historical community photos, newspaper clippings and artefacts.

■ **Elisha Kissick,**
owner of Yura Tours
@yura_tours

Left Island boardwalk
Above left Stradbroke Island beach
Above right Yura Tours (p194) guided walk

you can find an award-winning bush-tucker garden trail.

Yura Tours takes visitors to key cultural and historical sites on the island. On the three-hour guided excursion, Nunukul woman Elisha Kissick shares her family's stories and helps guests identify and taste bush tucker, including honey produced by native stingless bees.

For another contemporary perspective, stop into **Delvene Cockatoo-Collins' art studio** in Dunwich. Using techniques passed down from her grandmother, the Quandamooka artist produces ceramics, clothing and homewares with prints of *bunbiya* (turtles), *jalaman* (native bees) and *yalingbilla* (humpback whales).

Thar She Blows

Straddie is the easternmost point in Queensland, so thousands of humpback whales pass by during the winter months as they migrate to their Antarctic feeding grounds. The best vantage point to watch for them is from the 1.2km **Gorge Walk**

ⓘ Waterway Warnings

If you see ripples or waves on the surface of Brown Lake (Lake Bummiera), proceed with caution. According to Quandamooka stories, it's a sign that the rainbow serpent has travelled from her home in Blue Lake (Karboora) to play in its waters.

Like Bummiera, Karboora (meaning 'deep, silent pool') is a site of spiritual significance. To respect that, visitors are asked not to swim in Blue Lake regardless of the conditions. Instead, stick to the 5.2km walking track around its edges, and keep your eyes peeled for rare golden swamp wallabies, endemic to the island.

Left Blue Lake (Karboora) **Below** Gorge Walk

boardwalk at Point Lookout, which sits about 30m above sea level. You might also see dolphins, sea turtles and manta rays in the waters below, and koalas, eastern grey kangaroos and swamp wallabies in the surrounding bush.

Pure Shores

For many, the appeal of Straddie is having a wide stretch of sea and sand all to yourself. Main Beach is the spot for surf, patrolled Cylinder Beach is safe for swimming, and Frenchman's Beach is ideal for picnics.

But the freshwater lakes, perfect for a dip, are what truly set Minjerribah apart. **Brown Lake (Lake Bummiera)** may sound unappealing, but its waters are actually an inviting warm amber owing to tannins from the surrounding paperback eucalypts. It's not uncommon to see a koala on its shores. Or visit the freshwater **Myora Springs** at high tide, when seawater flows through the mangroves. Traditionally a favoured camping place of the Quandamooka people, the banks host large shell middens. You'll need a 4WD to access local favourite the **Keyholes**, just off Main Beach, or book a tour with 'barefoot' Dave from **Straddie Kingfisher Tours**. If you want to drive onto the beach in your own 4WD, you must purchase a permit online from Minjerribah Camping.

BUSH TUCKER
of Southeast Queensland

01
02
03
04
05

01 Davidson's plum
Only distantly related to European plums, *Davidsonia johnsonii* is too sour to be eaten raw. Instead, it's used in jams, wines and ice cream.

02 Native ginger
The rhizomes, young shoots and blue berries of this plant all have an earthy ginger flavour.

03 Native raspberry
Found in sunlit rainforest areas, these prickly bushes produce sweet red berries, which can be eaten raw or made into jam or tea.

04 Lemon myrtle
The leaves of this fragrant and flavourful herb also have handy mosquito-repelling properties.

05 Pigface
The salty leaves, fruit and flowers of this succulent – which grows on sand dunes – can be eaten raw or boiled.

06 Australian finger lime
This prized fruit is known as 'citrus caviar' for good reason. Squeeze out the segments for a burst of flavour.

07 Macadamia nut

Most of the world's macadamias are grown in Hawaii, but they're indigenous to Australia. Scientists believe they may originate from a single Queensland tree.

08 Bunya pine

Growing up to 50m, this tree produces a seed that can be eaten raw, roasted, or ground into flour for cakes.

09 Saltbush

An ingredient on menus at Australia's top restaurants, the salty leaves of this shrub are best fried.

10 Blue tongue

Not to be confused with the lizard of the same name, this evergreen has sweet blue fruit that will stain your mouth.

11 Native honey

This rare and intense sweet treat is produced by tiny stingless native bees, which are also called sugarbags.

36 Outback Noosa
CAMPING

CAMPING | SWIMMING | DOUGHNUTS

The go-to weekend destination for locals in the know, the small dairy-farming community of Kenilworth has a surprising number of drawcards for its size. Along the 1930s-era main street you'll find an award-winning cheese room and a fabulous bakery. But the real attraction is the surrounding rainforest, home to ancient fig trees and sublime swimming holes.

How to

Getting here & around A 25-minute drive inland from Eumundi, Kenilworth is easy to access. But to explore Conondale National Park you'll need a high-clearance 4WD.

When to go Avoid the crowds by visiting on a weekday. If you plan to swim, arrive after rain, when waterholes are fullest.

Don't get stung! Leaves of the giant stinging tree litter the rainforest floor in areas. Contact can result in stinging that lasts for hours or days.

Picnicking At **Kenilworth Country Bakery**, a doughnut as large as your head will cost you $20, but if you can eat the 1kg treat in one sitting, you'll get your money back. For basic picnic staples that won't send you into cardiac arrest, the sourdough loaves are just as satisfying. Get here early, as regular-size doughnuts often sell out before 1pm. Across the street, the cheese options at **Kenilworth Dairies** are overwhelming, so opt for the $10 sampler, with flavours such as lemon myrtle and macadamia.

Right top Creek crossing on the way to Booloumba Creek, Conondale National Park **Right bottom** Lemon myrtle and macadamia cheese, Kenilworth Dairies

STEPHANIE JACKSON - AUSTRALIAN LANDSCAPES/ALAMY STOCK PHOTO ©

LEEROY TODD PHOTOGRAPHY ©

🖼 Public Toilet as Public Art

Just outside town on the banks of the Mary River is Kenilworth's yellow-and-blue 'designer dunny'. *Canistrum*, Maleny architectural illustrator Michael Lennie's design, depicts an unfinished Aboriginal fishing basket, to reflect unfinished history.

A 13km drive southwest of Kenilworth is **Booloumba Creek** camping and day-use area in **Conondale National Park**. The crystal-clear water is refreshing on a hot day, with a rope swing to ease you in. You'll need a high-clearance 4WD to get here, unless you're willing to wade through the creek on foot. The start of the 3km bushwalk to **Booloumba Falls** is further along the 4WD track.

Camping Even if you don't have a 4WD, there's plenty of camping nearby. Five kilometres south of town, freedom camping spot Little Yabba Creek is the starting point for the **Giant Fig Tree** circuit. Or spend a night at **Kenilworth Homestead** to experience **Terra Firma**, an all-day event inspired by traditional Argentinian *asado* barbecues. Food is slow-cooked over an open flame before being served picnic-style. Buy tickets in advance, as it regularly sells out.

37

Seek Waterfalls & **WILDLIFE**

ROAD TRIP | PLATYPUSES | SHOPPING

The Sunshine Coast hinterland is only 30km from the ocean, but the region is a world apart from the hum of coastal activity. Ascend the Blackall Ranges to be rewarded with lush rainforests, green pastures, eclectic mountain towns and postcard-perfect views.

🧭 How to

Getting around It's a 23km drive from Mapleton to Maleny, but plan for plenty of stops. To extend your exploration, make it a circuit by taking Hwy 22 from Maleny to Kenilworth, taking Obi Obi Rd to Mapleton, and then returning to Maleny via Hwy 23.

When to go During the summer months the hinterland is cooler than the coast – and the waterfalls should be full and flowing.

Fill Your Belly & Your Bags

At the heart of the Sunshine Coast hinterland region are the townships of Maleny and Montville.

Appealing little **Montville** is known as the Blue Mountains of Queensland. Its buildings have a European Alps aesthetic, with storefronts mainly catering to visitors – which isn't necessarily a bad thing. There are numerous cafes, a chocolatier, a clockmaker, a tea shop and a handful of art galleries to explore.

Maleny is where locals from the surrounding area do their shopping – which is part of the reason you'll have a hard time finding parking. (Try behind the IGA.) Grab a coffee from Shotgun Espresso or a gelato from Maleny Food Co. to enjoy while wandering up the main street. Leave enough time to do

⛰️ One Tree Hill

Maleny's Mountain View Rd has unparalleled views of the Glass House Mountains, particularly from One Tree Hill, a popular photo stop. Located at 311 Mountain View Rd, the tree is on private land, so seek permission before entering. The entry fee ($50) goes to charity: more than $40,000 has been raised to date.

Left Clock shop, Montville **Above left** Kondalilla Falls (p202) **Above right** View from One Tree Hill, Maleny

the 900m walk to the Platypus Viewing Area, which can be found along the accessible boardwalk starting behind the Riverside Shopping Centre.

Further down the road is the village of **Mapleton**. Its pub, built in 1910, isn't known for its food but rather for its position – sitting at nearly 400m in elevation, it has a wrap-around verandah with clear views down to the coast and beyond.

Dive In

The ocean might be a half-hour drive away, but hinterland residents are spoilt for choice when it comes to wild swimming. One of the most accessible spots is at **Gardners Falls**, about 5km east of Maleny. From the car park, head downstream to find shady spots and rope swings. Another option is **Kondalilla Falls**, just southwest of Flaxton. For the best vantage point of the 90m drop, follow the

⊘ Platypus Whispers

You can find platypuses in the Mary River, in Peachester's creek and in Nambour, behind the train station. The national average is two platypuses for every kilometre of creek – but in Maleny's Obi Obi Creek, there are up to 10 per kilometre.

It's a misconception that platypuses are only active at dawn and dusk: they need to forage for up to 16 hours a day.

To spot them, look for a ring of low ripples on the water's surface that take a long time to dissipate. (By contrast, eastern water dragons produce very sharp ripples that dissipate quickly.)

■ **Neil Andison,** photographer, tour guide and platypus whisperer
www.facebook.com/platypus whisperer1

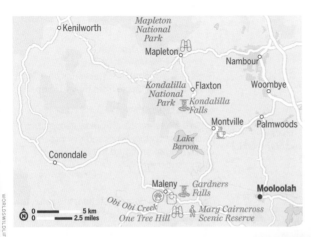

Left Platypus **Below** Mary Cairncross Scenic Reserve

4.7km-circuit bushwalk to the bottom of the falls – but note that the best swimming is in the rock pools at the top.

If you have ample time, the 58.8km **Sunshine Coast Hinterland Great Walk** takes about four days to complete. Starting from the dammed Lake Baroon, it passes by Kondalilla Falls, Baxter Falls, Mapleton Falls and Gheerulla Falls. Along the way, keep an eye out for yellow-tailed black cockatoos, snakes, goannas and, if you're lucky, koalas.

Ancient Remnants

When settlers arrived on the Sunshine Coast in the 1870s, they quickly set to work logging the area's red cedar and beech trees. The bush you see today is largely regrowth, with one notable exception: the 55-hectare **Mary Cairncross Scenic Reserve** outside Maleny. A remnant subtropical lowland rainforest, its trees have stood for hundreds of years, sheltering endemic species that you're unlikely to see elsewhere. The fully accessible trails provide an opportunity to spot red-legged pademelons, squirrel gliders, paradise riflebirds and rare plant species. Entry is by gold-coin donation, with interpreters on site to help you identify birdlife in the canopy.

Listings

BEST OF THE REST

Handmade Souvenirs

Birrunga Gallery

Not just an art gallery, this performance space and licensed wine bar is the only Indigenous-owned and -operated commercial cultural hub in Brisbane's CBD.

Artisan

Since 1970, Artisan has been the home of art and design in Queensland. Head to the store in Brisbane's Bowen Hills for Aboriginal textiles, opal jewellery and painted ceramics.

Pottery Studio

Learn to shape clay by hand, throw pottery on a wheel, glaze your work and fire up the kiln; locations in Maroochydore and Nambour.

David Linton Furniture & Timber Works

Showcasing the work of local artists, this expansive shop in Maleny sells beautifully carved objets d'art made from Australian woods, such as Huon pine and Bunya pine.

Family Fun

Bim'bimba Park

If there's one playground to rule them all, this would be it. This award-winning nature-based park in Pimpama has a 14m-high play tower and 3km of walking and cycling trails.

QAGOMA

The Queensland Art Gallery & Gallery of Modern Art are housed in two buildings in Brisbane. At the Kids' Art Centre, young artists can get their hands busy creating. Entry is free.

Glasshouse Plantation

Taste tropical fruits and macadamia nuts straight off the tree at this working farm in the Glass House Mountains. Weekends only; entry is free with a purchase from the gift shop.

Buderim Ginger Factory

Set in 9 hectares of subtropical garden, this place offers factory tours and tastings. Kids will love jumping aboard the 100-year-old sugar-cane train.

Mary Valley Rattler

Departing from Gympie Station, this refurbished steam train travels through the Mary Valley to the cute country communities of Dagun and Amamoor.

Distilleries & Drinks

Wild Flower

Distilling what it calls 'Burleigh in a bottle', the Gold Coast's Wild Flower produces gins and spirits, including speciality blends such as lamington-flavoured vodka.

Scenic Rim Brewery & Café $

Perfectly picturesque, this family-owned brewery is situated in the 100-year-old Mount Alford General Store. The beers pair perfectly with the Dutch home-style cooking.

Mary Valley Rattler

Howard Smith Wharves $$

Nestled under Brisbane's Story Bridge, along the historic wharves on the banks of the Brisbane River, are cocktail bars, restaurants and a brewery with wood-fired pizzas.

Piggyback $$

Run by Tony Kelly, known for Sunshine Coast institutions such as Rice Boi, Piggyback in Palmwoods serves up Asian street food and creative cocktails that diners queue for.

BeachTree Distilling Co.

Infusing native botanicals with organic and traditional ingredients, this Caloundra distillery makes animal-themed spirits, such as its Quokka gin. Tours can be arranged in advance.

🏪 Local Markets

Village Markets

This award-winning market is held at Burleigh Heads State School on the first and third Sunday of the month. Expect new and vintage clothing, homewares, jewellery and plants.

Collective Markets

Held Friday through Sunday on Little Stanley St in Brisbane's South Bank, these markets run into the evening hours, with food, live music and artisan fare.

Festive Fresh Market

One of Brisbane's longest-running fresh-food markets, Festive has over 200 stalls with an emphasis on produce, meat and baked goods.

Yandina Country Market

Best known for its massive selection of indoor and outdoor plants, this Saturday-morning market is where you can eyeball bush tucker and nosh on food from local vendors.

Eumundi Market

Legendary in southeast Queensland, this is allegedly the biggest artisan market in

Tallebudgera Creek

the country. It's open both Wednesday and Saturday; midweek is the quieter option.

☀ Sand & Surf

Tallebudgera Creek

With 70km of golden sand, there's no lack of swimming spots in the Gold Coast. A local family favourite, this estuary provides calm, warm waters for splashing, SUPing and kayaking.

Streets Beach

Brisbane may not be located on the ocean, but that doesn't mean it lacks a beach. This is Australia's only inner-city artificial beach, complete with white sand and subtropical plants.

Woorim Beach

The closest patrolled swimming and surfing beach to Brisbane, Bribie Island's family-friendly area has barbecues, picnic areas, playgrounds and a skate park nearby.

Mudjimba Beach

This long, unpatrolled stretch of sand is favoured by dog walkers. Wander through the Foreshore Conservation Reserve, which connects the ocean to the Maroochy River mouth.

 Scan to find more things to do in Brisbane & Southeast Queensland online

CAIRNS &
THE QUEENSLAND
COAST

REEF ADVENTURES | ANCIENT RAINFOREST | TROPICAL VIBES

Welcome to *Walu Wugirriga*

**Experience
Cairns & the
Queensland
Coast online**

*Gulf of
Carpentaria*

*Cape York
Peninsula*

*Daintree
National
Park*

*Great
Barrier
Reef*

Discover the top
sunset drinking
spots in **Cairns**
(p216)
✈ 2¼hrs from
Brisbane

*Staaten River
National Park*

*Wooroonooran
National Park*

Innisfail ●

*Bulleringa
National
Park*

Tully ●

Ingham ●

**Charters
Towers ●**

Mt Isa ●

Hughenden ●

QUEENSLAND

CAIRNS & THE QUEENSLAND COAST
Trip Builder

▬▬▬ The key gateway to the Great Barrier Reef
and the Daintree Rainforest, tropical Cairns is
an unmissable stop on any East Coast traveller's
itinerary. But the fun doesn't end here, with
waterfalls, reef adventures, Indigenous experiences
and more dotted all the way along the coast.

**Explore bookable
experiences in Cairns
& the Queensland
Coast online**

Visit the heart of
the Daintree at
Cape Tribulation
(p212)
🚗 1½hrs from
Cairns

*Coral
Sea*

*Hinchinbrook Island
National Park*

*South
Pacific
Ocean*

Go Barrier Reef Marine
Park island-hopping in
Townsville (p220)
🚗 4¼hrs from Cairns

*Bowling
Green Bay
National
Park*

● **Ayr**

● **Bowen**

● **Proserpine**

*Lake
Dalrymple*

*Eungella
National
Park*

● **Mackay**

● **Emerald**   ● **Blackwater**   ● **Rockhampton**

Walk in the footsteps of
the Butchulla people on
the **Fraser Coast** (p225)
🚗 3¼hrs from Brisbane

● **Gladstone**

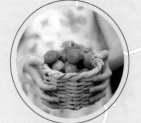

Eat your way around
the food bowl of
Bundaberg (p226)
🚗 4½hrs from
Brisbane

*Fraser Island,
Great Sandy
National Park*

*Fraser
Island*

● **Hervey
Bay**

Practicalities

CHAMELEONSEYE/SHUTTERSTOCK ©

ARRIVING

Cairns Airport Busy domestic and international airport 5km north of the city centre. A taxi costs around $20. Transfers to Cairns and Port Douglas are available with Excellence Coaches; book ahead or enquire at the arrivals hall desk.

Townsville Airport Receives flights from major Australian and regional Queensland cities.

Bundaberg Regional Airport Serviced by QantasLink. Pick up a hire car here, or take a shuttle (book ahead) or taxi.

HOW MUCH FOR A

NP camping site per person $7

Pub meal $10-25

Barrier Reef day trip $200-270

GETTING AROUND

Hire car A car is by far the easiest way to explore the region, where many attractions lie off public-transport routes. Check your insurance coverage before heading along unsealed roads.

Bus All major towns have some sort of public bus network. Greyhound Australia offers hop-on, hop-off tickets for routes between Cairns and Melbourne (starting at $199 for seven days).

Walking Northern tourism hubs including Cooktown, Port Douglas, Cairns and Townsville are relatively easy to get around on foot. Wear sun protection and stay hydrated.

WHEN TO GO

JUN–OCT
The dry, cool season offers ideal weather for outdoor activities

OCT–DEC
You might be lucky to catch the annual coral spawning

NOV–MAR
See marine turtles nest and hatch on Great Barrier Reef beaches

NOV–MAY
Bargains can be found during the wet, humid season

EATING & DRINKING

The further north you travel, the more likely you are to find barramundi (a tender, white-flesh fish; pictured right) on menus. Many coastal pubs offer a different $15 meal special each night. And while fine dining is less common, there are several standouts to be discovered. Craft beers, along with boutique spirits, now have a foothold in northern Queensland, but it's a rite of passage to try to finish a schooner of XXXX. Good coffee is now easier to find, particularly in Cairns.

Best cocktails
Three Wolves (p217)

Best food market
Rusty's Market (p231; pictured right)

CONNECT & FIND YOUR WAY

Wi-fi Complimentary at most accommodation, but less commonly available at cafes. The best way to stay connected is to purchase a local SIM card; reception can be patchy to non-existent outside cities and larger towns.

Navigation Download offline maps to save your mobile data. Maps.me tends to have good walking-trail coverage. The Queensland National Parks & Wildlife Service has downloadable trail-map pdfs.

WHERE TO STAY

Road-trippers will find plenty of waterside holiday parks and scenic national-park campgrounds along the coast. Resort bargains abound in Cairns and Port Douglas during the wet season.

Location	Atmosphere
Cairns & Port Douglas	Resorts galore, with more hotel and hostel options in Cairns.
Cassowary Coast	Camping, motels & B&Bs.
Townsville	Hotels, holiday apartments and a few hostels.
Whitsundays	Flash island resorts; affordable resorts, hotels and hostels on the mainland.
Capricorn Coast, Bundaberg & Fraser Coast	Family-friendly resorts and holiday parks, B&Bs and small hotels.

STINGER SAFETY

Marine stingers are present along the northern Queensland coast (down to around Fraser Island) from November to May; protective stinger suits are provided by activity operators.

MONEY

Cash is more readily accepted up here than it is further south – handy when Eftpos machines drop offline in bad weather or in remote locations. Smaller towns may not have ATMs.

38 Escape to CAPE TRIB

DAINTREE RAINFOREST | ROAD TRIP | SWIMMING HOLES

When you drive off the ferry that shuttles vehicles across the Daintree River, it feels like you've entered another realm. The Daintree Rainforest and the Great Barrier Reef meet at Cape Tribulation ('Cape Trib'), a magical place dotted with rainforest trails and freshwater swimming holes. Most visitors only come for a day, but it's worth carving out three to connect more deeply with this off-grid wonder.

AUSTRALIANCAMERA/SHUTTERSTOCK ©

🗺 How to

Getting here & around
The Daintree Ferry is a 1½-hour drive north of Cairns. Once across, it's about an hour to Kulki Lookout at the cape's northern end (if you don't stop).

When to go Avoid (most of) the rain during the May–November dry season.

Where to stay More than a dozen guesthouses (some with their own natural swimming holes) dot Cape Trib. Several camping spots include a basic national-park camp-ground at Noah Beach.

MICHAEL SMITH (TWP)/SHUTTERSTOCK ©

Emmagen Creek
Kulki
Lookout
Great
Barrier Reef
Mackay
Reef
°Cape Tribulation
Mason's
Swimming
Hole
Daintree
National
Park
Undine
Reef
Madja
Boardwalk

Rudder
Reef

○Cow Bay
Jindalba Circuit
Track

0 —— 5 km
0 —— 2.5 miles

CAIRNS & THE QUEENSLAND COAST EXPERIENCES

Far left top Boardwalk, Daintree
National Park **Far left bottom**
Marine turtle

Nature's Playground

Rainforest trails Overnight stays allow for tackling Cape
Trib's longer walks, including the lush Jindalba Circuit Track
(3km) and the 7km-return slog up Mt Sorrow for spectacular
views (allow six hours). Weaving through coastal mangroves,
the elevated Madja Boardwalk (1.2km) is one of the world's
most scenic wheelchair-accessible trails. Learn more about
this ancient ecosystem on a walk with long-time local Neil
Hewett (coopercreek.com.au). Cassowaries are spotted on
most of his tours.

Next-level snorkelling If you only do one Great Barrier Reef
snorkelling tour, make it this one. It only takes 25 minutes on
Ocean Safari's inflatable boat to reach Mackay and Undine
Reefs. Part of the Great Barrier Reef, these neighbouring reefs
teem with marine turtles, tropical fish and some of the most
beautiful, untouched corals accessible to snorkellers in the
entire World Heritage Site. Gin-clear waters and shallow reef
systems create ideal conditions for underwater photography.

Magical waterholes Cape Trib's beautiful beaches are off
limits for swimming due to salties, but some of Australia's
best (and croc-safe) freshwater swimming holes are found
here. Don't miss Emmagen Creek (3.5km along the Bloomfield Track) and Mason's Swimming Hole (behind Mason's
Cafe; gold-coin – $1 or $2 – donation). There's another
beautiful waterhole you may hear about but won't find sign-
posted, and for good reason: it's a sacred site for Kuku Yalanji
Traditional Owners.

⌖ 4WD Adventure

One of Australia's most
legendary 4WD trails, the
Bloomfield Track links the
northern end of Cape Trib
to the Aboriginal commu-
nity of Wujal Wujal, from
where a sealed road runs
to Cooktown. The Bloom-
field is only 30km long, but
it's a famously challenging
drive, with creek crossings,
ultra-steep hills, and
potholes the size of
people. An extra 40km
past Wujal Wujal (don't
miss its Indigenous arts
centre), the historic Lion's
Den Hotel is an obligatory
post-Bloomfield stop. If
one celebratory beer turns
into a few – which can
easily happen here – you
can camp on the property.
The pizzas are excellent.

Daintree Dreaming

FEEL THE ANCIENT ENERGY

An ecosystem so spectacular that Sir David Attenborough called it 'the most extraordinary place on Earth', the Daintree Rainforest is a real-life Jurassic Park, home to descendants of plants and animals from the era of the dinosaurs. This biodiversity powerhouse is not only ecologically significant but also culturally important to its Traditional Owners, the Eastern Kuku Yalanji rainforest people.

Left Daintree rainforest **Middle** Magnificent tree frog **Right** Southern cassowary

AUSTRALIANCAMERA/SHUTTERSTOCK ©

Covering more than 1200 sq km between Mossman Gorge and the Bloomfield River, the otherworldly Daintree is estimated to be around 180 million years old. So it's no wonder that visiting this verdant corner of Queensland feels like stepping (way) back in time.

Part of the Wet Tropics World Heritage Area (WTWHA), the ancient rainforest is also protected by Daintree National Park, which has two sections: Mossman Gorge and Cape Tribulation. Just 20 minutes from Port Douglas, the Mossman Gorge Centre at the national park's southern end is the most accessible section. Here you can take self-guided or Indigenous-led walks and swim in the idyllic Mossman River, which tumbles between huge granite boulders. On the northern side of the Daintree River, accessed by a car ferry, the Cape Tribulation section (p212; 110km north of Cairns) feels even more wild, but like Mossman Gorge it also has a handful of easily accessible walking trails, as well as accommodation and ecotours.

Historic Handback

In 2021, more than 1600 sq km of land in Tropical North Queensland, including the Daintree Rainforest, was officially handed back to Eastern Kuku Yalanji people.

Central to the culture and spirituality of the Eastern Kuku Yalanji, who have an intimate knowledge of the rainforest passed down through generations, the handback means that Daintree National Park will now be jointly managed by Traditional Owners and the Queensland government. The specifics were still being nutted out at the time of research,

but the handback is expected to create fresh opportunities for tourism in the national park, with planning for a cultural hub already under way.

Heritage Under Threat

Having survived for so long, the Daintree might seem pretty resilient. But research has found that the WTWHA, home to 36% of Australia's mammal species alone, is highly susceptible to climate change. Current modelling predicts that global warming of just 1°C – expected to occur within the next decade – will produce a decrease of 60% in the distributional range of the region's endemic vertebrate species. At 3.5°C, approximately 65% of endemic vertebrates are projected to disappear from the WTWHA, leading to a strong likelihood of mass extinctions, beginning with frogs and possums.

> The otherworldly Daintree is estimated to be around 180 million years old. So it's no wonder that visiting this verdant corner of Queensland feels like stepping back in time.

Additional threats to the rainforest identified by the Wet Tropics Management Authority include invasive species such as feral pigs and yellow crazy ants, increased demand for infrastructure, and a significant decline in research and investment due to a lack of government funding. And while tourism, too, has the potential to create negative impacts, it's impossible to visit this special place without being inspired to help protect it.

🏠 Daintree Experiences

Rainforest lodges Immerse yourself in the rainforest by staying at a rainforest lodge at Cape Tribulation or near Mossman Gorge, such as the recently reopened, ecofriendly Silky Oaks Lodge.

Croc cruise Operating on the Daintree River, Solar Whisper boats are both ecofriendly and super-quiet, so you can glide up to crocodiles and other wildlife without scaring the animals.

Daintree Discovery Centre In the Cape Tribulation section, this attraction has a treetop walkway that immerses you in the canopy – look out for cassowaries down below.

Indigenous experiences See p222 for more information.

39 Sundowners in CAIRNS

CRAFT COCKTAILS | SEA VIEWS | GOOD TIMES

████ With year-round balmy weather, the buzzy Tropical North Queensland holiday hub of Cairns was made for sunset drinks by the sea. The city's bar scene has exploded in recent years, with craft breweries joined by slick rooftop bars and moody laneway speakeasies.

OCHRE RESTAURANT AND CATERING ©

🍴 Dinner Time

Ochre Restaurant (pictured) Cairns' best waterfront fine dining, with creative uses of native ingredients.

Tokyo Dumpling Serves the best Japanese curry outside Japan.

CC's Bar & Grill Ideal for date night, with a high-end fit-out and top-quality steaks.

🗺 Trip Notes

Getting around The bars of central Cairns are all within easy walking distance.

Don't miss Near Cairns Airport, the Stratford neighbourhood is an emerging drinking hub; here Barrier Reef Brewing Co. was recently joined by the Fox Small Bar and Narrow Tracks Distilling, which opens its tasting room on Friday and Saturday afternoons.

Happy hour Cairns' bars offer great happy-hour deals, but Queensland law prohibits advertising them externally. Contact venues for current deals.

■ **Tips by Darren Barber,** *co-owner of the Hospo Group (which includes Three Wolves and the Fox Small Bar)* @darrenjbarber

01 Start on a high – literally, at Cairns' most elevated bar. Perched on the 12th-floor rooftop of the Crystalbrook Riley hotel, Mediterranean-inspired **Rocco** calls for an Aperol spritz (or two).

03 With a prime location on Cairns' marina, swanky **Salt House** is a superb spot to watch the sun go down with a cocktail in hand.

Stratford (8km)

Minnie St.

Abbott St.

Esplanade

Cairns Harbour

Pier Marina

02 Soak up more epic Coral Sea sunset views at **Whiskey & Wine**, on level two of the Riley's sister hotel Flynn, where you can choose from more than 80 local and imported whiskies.

Aplin St.

Abbott St.

Lake St.

Pierpoint Rd.

Marlin Marina

05 You won't be able to see the sunset from **Three Wolves**, but you'll be happy you found this Prohibition-inspired laneway bar when you sample its theatrical cocktails.

C A I R N S

Spence St.

Wharf St.

McLeod St.

Grafton St.

Bunda St.

Sheridan St.

Hartley St.

Wharf St.

🚉 Cairns Central

Trinity Inlet

HEMINGWAY'S BREWERY

04 When only a craft beer will do, **Hemingway's Brewery** is the place to pair a frothy one with views across Chinaman Creek towards the forested peaks of the Great Dividing Range.

WILDLIFE OF THE
Wet Tropics World Heritage Area

01 Ulysses butterfly
Seen throughout the region, particularly in Cape Tribulation, the star of the Wet Tropics' insect world has huge, electric-blue wings.

02 Amethystine python
Named for the irides-cent sheen on its scales, Australia's largest snake is as beautiful as it is docile.

03 Spotted-tailed quoll
The famously elusive ground-dwelling predator is mainland Australia's second-largest native carnivore, after the dingo.

04 Lace monitor
Known to skulk around campgrounds looking for an easy snack, these beautifully patterned lizards can grow up to 1.5m long

05 Boyd's forest dragon
Look for these colourful, myth-like 'dragons' clinging to tree trunks along the pathways of Mossman Gorge.

06 Herbert River ringtail possum
Affectionately known as 'Herbie', the nocturnal emblem of the Queensland Parks & Wildlife Service is found at highland altitudes.

07 Mahogany glider

Increasingly threatened by land clearing, this endangered sweet-toothed glider is one of six glider species found in the Wet Tropics.

08 Tree kangaroo

Two arboreal kangaroo species live in the Wet Tropics. Try your luck spotting the Lumholtz's tree kangaroo in the Atherton Tablelands.

09 Southern cassowary

The dinosaur-like icon of the Wet Tropics faces an uncertain future, with fewer than 1000 estimated to remain in the wild.

10 Musky rat-kangaroo

This adorable pint-sized 'roo is diurnal, meaning it can often be seen foraging on the forest floor during the day.

11 Platypus

Sit quietly by Peterson Creek in Yungaburra in the Atherton Tablelands at dawn or dusk for good chances of observing these monotremes.

12 Saltwater crocodile

The world's largest living reptile patrols the rivers and beaches of the Wet Tropics and beyond.

40 Townsville Island HOPS

ISLAND HIKING | BEACHES | INDIGENOUS CULTURE

■■■■ With the final stages of the Museum of Underwater Art (MOUA) in development at Magnetic and Palm Islands, there's a great new reason to visit these lesser-known Great Barrier Reef isles. Also the gateway to MOUA's pièce de résistance, the Coral Greenhouse, Townsville is preparing to reopen its premier marine attraction, the Reef HQ Aquarium, in 2023 following a major upgrade.

🗺 How to

Getting here & around
Magnetic Island Ferries (which takes cars) and SeaLink run daily services from Townsville to Magnetic Island (25 to 40 minutes). SeaLink runs to Palm Island Wednesday to Monday (one hour 45 minutes). Miniature 'Barbie

Cars' can be rented on Magnetic Island.

When to go May to September, when the humidity's lower and stinger suits aren't required.

Snorkel Great options at Magnetic Island beyond MOUA include the snorkel trails at Nelly Bay and Geoffrey Bay.

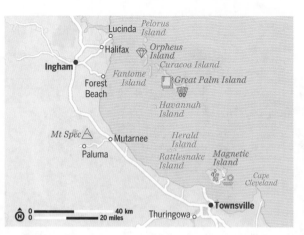

Far left top Horseshoe Bay, Magnetic Island **Far left bottom** Jetty, Orpheus Island

Magnetic Island Laid-back 'Maggie' boasts palm-fringed beaches, good snorkelling, scenic hiking trails and a robust koala population. Taking you to WWII fortifications with epic views (with koala-spotting on the way), the 4km-return Forts Walk is the island's top trail. Pack a picnic and continue from Forts Junction around to Horseshoe Bay via Radical Bay, a 7.5km trail linking the island's most beautiful beaches. Come for the day or stay longer, with plenty of holiday accommodation to choose from.

Palm Island Best known for its troubled history, the former Aboriginal mission of Palm Island (Bwgcolman) is now looking to tourism to future-proof its economy. The biggest development is the local instalment of MOUA, with day trips from Townsville with SeaLink ferries also on the agenda. There's talk of a dive centre opening on the rustic, rainforest-clad island. Local Indigenous guides can take you to cultural sites and remote snorkelling spots.

Orpheus Island The only way to get to this private island retreat in the Palm Island group is by helicopter as a guest of luxe Orpheus Island Lodge, which welcomes a maximum of 28 guests at any one time. Spend your days snorkelling (the Great Barrier Reef's widest boulder coral was discovered here in 2021), kayaking or sailing just offshore, or take a boat trip to the outer reef.

ⓘ Plan Your Palm Island Visit

Etiquette For independent visits, it's best to contact the local council to let them know you're coming. They can connect you with guides and provide information about visiting respectfully.

Whale watching In July and August you can often spot migrating humpback whales on the boat trip to Palm Island from Townsville. If the whales are close, the boat stops for a while to let you watch.

Culture Start your visit at the Bwgcolman Indigenous Knowledge Centre, near the jetty, for a primer on local culture. We have lots of celebrations during Naidoc Week in July, so that's a good time to come to experience culture.

■ **Vicki Saylor,** *Manbarra Traditional Owner and cultural adviser* @vickeranne

41 Through Indigenous EYES

TOURS | BUSH TUCKER | CULTURE

More than 70 Aboriginal and Torres Strait Islander groups have lived alongside the Great Barrier Reef for millennia. There have never been more opportunities to explore the region with Indigenous guides, particularly in the following tourism hubs.

CULTURE CONNECT PTY LTD ©

📷 How to

Etiquette Always ask before taking photos on an Indigenous-led tour, as it may not be allowed for cultural reasons. And remember that no question is too silly if it's asked respectfully.

More Discover and book more Indigenous experiences via the Welcome to Country website (welcometo country.com).

Eat Enjoy a sumptuous seven-course dinner featuring native ingredients at the Aboriginal Cultural Experience, run by Aboriginal-owned Flames of the Forest, near Port Douglas.

Cooktown

The first recorded act of reconciliation between Indigenous and non-Indigenous people in Australia occurred in Cooktown. This is just one of the fascinating facts you'll learn on a self-guided tour of the **James Cook Museum**, which recounts Captain Cook's landing here in June 1770 from an Aboriginal perspective. Then head out on Country with guide Willie Gordon of **Guurrbi Tours** to see rock art and gain insight into local Aboriginal society and spirituality. Or sign up for a rock art and ranger tour with **Culture Connect**, which will take you deep into Balngarrawarra Country, west of Cooktown, to see ancient rock art and visit land-restoration projects helping to protect the Great Barrier Reef.

Cairns & Daintree

Cairns' first Indigenous-led Great Barrier Reef tour, **Dreamtime Dive & Snorkel** weaves Indigenous storytelling, music and

Left James Cook Museum
Above left Culture Connect Aboriginal rock art tour

dance throughout its day trip. Opened in 2022, a new pontoon at Moore Reef has created additional opportunities to interact with Indigenous 'sea ranger' guides, and learn more about how Indigenous knowledge and science are helping to protect the world's largest living ecosystem.

Nearby, in the Daintree region – the traditional home of Eastern Kuku Yalanji people – there are a number of Indigenous experiences. On a Ngadiku Dreamtime Walk,

organised by the Indigenous-run **Mossman Gorge Centre**, your guide will tell you more about the special relationship their people share with the unique tropical environment during a meandering rainforest stroll. You can also explore the Daintree region with Kuku Yalanji guides from **Walkabout Cultural Adventures**. Or take a cultural walk along Cooya Beach near Mossman with brothers Linc and Brandon Walker of **Kuku Yalanji Cultural Habitat Tours**. Feeling creative? Sign up for

📖 Indigenous Must-Reads

Dark Emu, by Bruce Pascoe (2014) Re-examining colonial accounts of Indigenous people in Australia, this groundbreaking non-fiction tome challenges long-held perceptions of Australia's first peoples.

Welcome to Country: A Travel Guide to Indigenous Australia, by Marcia Langton (2018) Cultural etiquette tips, plus insights into Aboriginal languages, customs, art and more.

The Yield, by Tara June Winch (2019) Evocative tale of a man's determination to preserve his people's language and culture. Winner of the coveted Miles Franklin Literary Award in 2020.

Australia Day, by Stan Grant (2019) Excellent backgrounder on Aboriginal Australia, with uncomfortable truths about the country's colonial history.

📷 Indigenous Art

The mid-year Cairns Indigenous Art Fair offers an unrivalled opportunity to purchase Indigenous art and handicrafts directly from artists. Throughout the year, northern Queensland's Indigenous art centres, such as the Yarrabah Art Centre, near Cairns, as well as the Cairns Art Gallery, host excellent exhibitions.

an art class with renowned Aboriginal artist Brian 'Binna' Swindley at **Janbal Gallery**.

Townsville

A central theme in Indigenous culture, caring for Country (traditional lands) is woven into each instalment of the Townsville region's **Museum of Underwater Art** (MOUA). On dry land, **Gudjuda Tours** runs an immersive bush-tucker tour in the Townsville region. Its owners, the Gudjuda Reference Group Aboriginal Corporation, have been conducting marine-turtle tagging and monitoring for more than 20 years. In 2022 the corporation launched a 'turtle rodeo' tour, offering visitors a chance to help collect valuable data that's used to inform turtle conservation.

Fraser Coast

Walk in the footsteps of a Butchulla man on the **Djinang Cultural Walking Tour** in Hervey Bay. Learn more about significant sites to the Butchulla people in Hervey Bay and nearby K'gari (Fraser Island), and sample local bush tucker, and get creative using natural materials. The tour is run in partnership with Hervey Bay Eco Marine Tours, which also runs a cultural sunset cruise with a Butchulla guide on board.

Left Rainforest walk, Mossman Gorge Centre **Above top** Cairns Indigenous Art Fair **Above** Costumed Torres Strait Island dancer, Cairns

42 Bundaberg's
BOUNTY

FOOD TRAILS | RUM | FARM GATES

Australia's food bowl, Bundaberg grows 25% of Australia's fresh produce. And there are more opportunities than ever to sample the bounty of this friendly farming region directly from the source, from fresh fruit to rum and spirits crafted with local sugar cane and botanicals.

ALEX CIMBAL/SHUTTERSTOCK ©

⬚ How to

Getting here & around Bundaberg is a 4½-hour drive (or a longer bus ride) north of Brisbane. The more scenic Queensland Rail Tilt Train takes 4½ hours. You'll need your own wheels to visit farm gates; hire-car options are plentiful.

When to go Year-round; Bundaberg Tourism's produce calendar details what's in season (bundabergregion.org).

Stay Recently opened Splitters Farm offers camping and glamping, and a menagerie of rescued farm animals to meet.

THE POCKET STOREHOUSE ©

Distilleries & Drinks

Producing liquid gold since 1889, **Bundaberg Rum** is a local icon. Even if you're not a 'Bundy' drinker, the distillery tour is fascinating, particularly the museum, with each section housed in a retired 75,000L vat. There's also a blend-your-own-rum experience.

But Bundaberg Rum is no longer the only distillery in town. Visits to the cellar door of artisanal distiller **Kalki Moon** include two tastings – gin is its key tipple, but there are also vodka and liqueurs, with rum on the way. Learn more on a tour with head distiller Rick Prosser, or kick back with a cocktail in the huge bar or gin garden.

You can also sample locally brewed Bargara Brewing Company craft beers at the city-centre brewhouse now known as **Ballistic Bargara**,

☼ Early Riser

Only open 9am to 2pm Thursday and 7am to noon Saturday, teeny bakery the **Pocket Storehouse** turns out some of the finest sourdough you'll ever sample. The fermentation process of its authentic, organic sourdough renders the bread essentially gluten-free, making it popular among coeliacs (though not officially recommended).

LEEROY TODD ©

Left Kalki Moon gins **Above left** Bundaberg Rum Distillery **Above right** Sourdough loaves, Pocket Storehouse

and taste the flavours of Bundaberg at the home of boutique drinks brand **Ohana Winery and Cheeky Tiki Cider**. Run by a local couple, Ohana/Cheeky Tiki specialises in tropical wines and ciders, and liqueurs made with regional produce – the likes of strawberry Moscato and pineapple cider.

Housed in a giant barrel, **Bundaberg Brewed Drinks** produces premium soft drinks from Queensland ingredients, from ginger to mango. Taste your way through the range and create your own six pack as part of the self-guided gallery tour.

Farm-Gate Experiences

Learn about the sustainable farming practices of family-run **Macadamias Australia** and sample its premium nuts at its visitor centre, opened in 2021, which has an attached boutique and a pleasant cafe overlooking a macadamia orchard.

🐟 Indigenous Food

Before Bundaberg's modern farmers arrived, Taribelang people fished, hunted and farmed the region's natural bounty. Learn more on a 2½-hour tour of Taribelang Country with recently launched Taribelang Bunda Cultural Tours.

'We've always eaten a lot of seafood here, from fish to pipis', says tour guide Rebecca Domaille. 'But also kangaroo, which is usually cooked on hot coals, and go-anna, which we might steam in paperbark'.

The cultural tour includes a taste of local bush tucker in the form of fresh damper with bush-tomato relish or lilly-pilly and lemon-myrtle jam. 'We're also develop-ing an Aboriginal dining experience at a culturally significant lookout'.

■ With Rebecca Domaille, *Taribelang woman and tour guide*

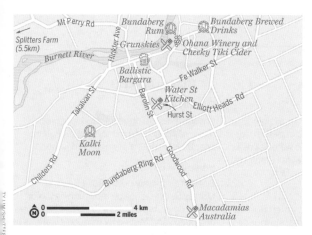

Left Bundaberg Brewed Drinks beverages **Below** Freshly harvested macadamias

Pick your own strawberries at **Tinaberries** from August to early October, or pop by at any time of the year to sample the farm's gourmet strawberry and passion-fruit ice creams. You can also shop for a wide range of fresh produce at farm gates including **Alloway Farm Market**, the **Lettuce Patch**, and **Our Little Farm**, which also sells delicious salads and frittatas, making it a great light lunch option.

Paddock-to-Plate Dining

Fresh Bundaberg produce is championed at local restaurants and cafes, with must-visits including the **Windmill Cafe** in the satellite suburb of Bargara, arguably one of Queensland's best brunch spots (tip: the açai bowl with local dragon fruit will feed two). Come dinner time, chef Alex Cameron whips Bundaberg's finest produce into modern Australian dishes that look as good as they taste at **Water St Kitchen**, hidden in a residential neighbourhood.

Bundaberg's fresh produce also includes seafood, which is hauled off the trawlers at **Grunskies**' own wharf. This Bundaberg institution has a seafood market attached to its restaurant overlooking the Burnett River, where you can feast on locally caught prawns, reef fish and more.

Listings

BEST OF THE REST

 Wondrous Waterfalls

Barron Falls

Take the elevated, wheelchair-accessible Barron Falls Lookout Track (1.2km return) for a front-on view of this dramatic waterfall near Kuranda. Or view it from the Skyrail Rainforest Cableway or Kuranda Scenic Railway.

Millaa Millaa Waterfall

Arguably the most photogenic waterfall in the Atherton Tablelands, near Cairns, surrounded by lush rainforest.

Josephine Falls

The crystal-clear pool at the bottom of this cascade in Wooroonooran National Park, an hour's drive south of Cairns, is one of Queensland's most idyllic freshwater swimming spots. It's a 1.2km return walk from the car park.

Wallaman Falls

Southwest of Ingham in Girringun National Park, the highest permanent single-drop waterfall in Australia plunges 268m into the gorge below. There's a viewing platform on the edge of the gorge, from where you can hike down to the base of the falls.

Little Crystal Creek

Cascading under a heritage-listed stone arch bridge, this series of small waterfalls is a picturesque spot to cool off in Paluma Range National Park, near Townsville.

Finch Hatton Gorge

Hike alongside a turquoise cascade tumbling through Finch Hatton Gorge in Eungella National Park, an hour's drive west of Mackay. There are natural swimming pools at the ends of the Wheel of Fire Track (4.2km return) and the Araluen Cascades Track (2.8km return).

 Hidden Beaches

Etty Bay Beach

Cassowaries are often spotted foraging on this small beach surrounded by rainforest near Innisfail. Has a popular campground.

Horseshoe Bay Beach

Linked to similarly pretty Rose Bay and Murray Bay beaches by the stunning 2.5km Cape Edgecumbe Walking Trail, this tiny curve of golden sand fringed by turquoise water is a gorgeous place for a swim in Bowen.

Coral Beach

Take the 1.1km rainforest track in Conway National Park, east of Airlie Beach, to this secluded coral rubble beach.

Cape Hillsborough Beach

It's famous for its kangaroos that gather on the beach at dawn, attracted by 'roo food provided by the local council, but this remote beach is a beautiful spot for a stroll at any time of day. For great views, hike up the Andrews Point Track at the southern end of the beach (5.2km return).

Kuranda Scenic Railway and Barron Falls

Springs Beach

Enjoy a dip at picturesque Springs Beach, just south of Agnes Water, or head south along the trail linking it to Red Rock Beach to find a series of small coves and rock pools.

 ## Epic Food Markets

Rusty's Market $

Cairns' iconic tropical fresh produce market (Friday to Sunday) is surrounded by street-food stalls.

 ## Seaside Pubs

Court House Hotel $$

Housed in a gorgeous old Queenslander on Wharf St, 'The Courty' in Port Douglas oozes old-school Aussie pub charm. The premium location has prices to match.

Mission Beach Tavern $$

A block from Mission Beach, this relaxed neighbourhood pub serves good-value classic pub grub, from mackerel and chips to chicken parmigiana. It's just a 200m stroll from Mission Beach Camping & Caravan Park.

Dingo Beach Hotel $$

Right on Dingo Beach, a 40-minute drive north of Airlie Beach in the Whitsundays, this relaxed, unassuming pub is a choice spot to while away an afternoon with a coldie in hand.

Eimeo Pacific Hotel $$

Perched at the edge of a cliff in Mackay's northern suburbs with cracking views towards the Cumberland Islands, this historic pub is a fantastic lunch spot.

1770 Beach Hotel $$

Ease into the relaxed vibe of Seventeen Seventy at this rustic pub, just paces from the peaceful 1770 Inlet Beach.

Big Mango

Bargara Beach Hotel $$

Tucked behind the esplanade on the Bundaberg coast, the recently renovated Bargara Beach Hotel has a sweeping deck, craft brews and an extensive pub-grub menu.

Quirky Attractions

Historic Village Herberton

With more than 50 restored period buildings, this outdoor museum is an unmissable Atherton Tablelands attraction.

Paronella Park

This tropical pleasure garden, south of Cairns, has a Spanish castle built by emigrant José Paronella in the 1930s.

Big Mango

You can't miss the 10m-high mango statue on the Bruce Hwy in Bowen. The next-door Bowen Visitor Information Centre sells mango ice cream.

Capricorn Caves

Just 30 minutes north of Gladstone, this series of beautiful limestone caves can be visited on three types of guided tour.

 Scan to find more things to do in Cairns & the Queensland Coast online

43 Discovering
THE REEF

DIVING | ISLANDS | CONSERVATION

With 2300km of the Great Barrier Reef (GBR) to explore, where does a traveller begin? Hint: the outer reef is generally the best place to snorkel and dive, from top to bottom. Pinpoint your perfect base with this quick guide.

🔲 How to

Getting here It takes around 90 minutes to reach the outer reef on a motorised catamaran from Port Douglas and Cairns, and around two hours from Townsville and Bundaberg.

When to go The comfortably warm May–October dry season

proffers the best conditions for diving and snorkelling, though many operators run trips year-round.

Reef-safe sunscreen Protect the reef by using sunscreens that contain only mineral UV-blocking ingredients such as oxide and titanium dioxide.

Northern Great Barrier Reef

Stretching from the Torres Strait to Hinchinbrook Island, north of Townsville, the Northern GBR is typically accessed from the holiday resort hubs of Cairns and Port Douglas, with smaller operators running trips from Cape Tribulation and Mission Beach. Or base yourself on luxe Lizard Island, reached by plane.

Visitors are spoilt for choice when it comes to reef operators. While bigger boats offer a smoother ride, you'll share the reef with more people. Day and overnight trips to Green and Fitzroy Islands are also possible from Cairns.

While you may encounter some bleaching on northern reefs, which are more susceptible to extreme weather events including cyclones and heatwaves, tourist boats visit some of the healthiest corners of the marine park, which

tend to have more vibrant corals than the southern, more temperate end of the reef.

Despite ongoing threats to the reef – climate change being the biggest – the World Heritage

Left Beaked coralfish **Above left** Lady Musgrave Island (p235)

site received some good news in 2021 from the Australian Institute of Marine Science, which found that coral cover was rising in all three areas.

Central Great Barrier Reef

The Central GBR runs from the Townsville region down to Mackay, with outer-reef day trips available from Townsville, Orpheus Island, Magnetic Island, Airlie Beach, the Whitsundays and Mackay.

The Townsville region is home to the Museum of Underwater Art (MOUA) as well as the SS *Yongala*, Australia's best wreck dive. There's decent snorkelling around the islands of the Central GBR, but this region doesn't compare to the quality of outer-reef locations like Hardy Reef. Visited by Cruise Whitsundays day trips from Airlie and the Whitsundays, Hardy Reef's Reefworld Pontoon also has two underwater hotel rooms (Reefsuites) and an upper-deck camping experience (Reefsleep).

♡ Give Back to the Reef

Get involved with citizen science. Every visitor can help to safeguard the reef by uploading data via the Eye on the Reef app.

Visit the reef with a High Standard Operator (see gbrmpa.gov.au); many have a Master Reef Guide on board.

Support reef-friendly businesses; most are Advanced Ecotourism certified by Ecotourism Australia.

Join the Citizens of the Great Barrier Reef by making an online pledge to take reef-friendly actions at home.

Follow the Reef Authority's motto: See the Reef, Love the Reef, Protect the Reef.

■ **David Wachenfeld,** *Chief Scientist, Great Barrier Reef Marine Park Authority* @ReefChiefSci

Turtles Ahoy!

Mon Repos Turtle Centre
From November, nightly ranger-led tours observe marine turtles coming ashore near Bundaberg to lay their eggs. Hatchlings appear from January to late March.

Cairns Turtle Rehabilitation Centre This Fitzroy Island centre cares for sick and injured turtles. Book a turtle tour to meet the patients.

Southern Great Barrier Reef

Ending at Lady Elliot Island, home to the reef's foremost eco-resort, the lesser-visited southern fringe of the GBR has much to offer. New on the scene is the Lady Musgrave HQ, a pontoon anchored near uninhabited Lady Musgrave Island on the outer reef that's used as a base for day and overnight trips from Bundaberg. The calm, shallow lagoon is fantastic for families.

Lady Musgrave Island day trips are also available from Seventeen Seventy, while overnight stays on Heron Island and nearby Wilson Island depart from Gladstone. Closer to the mainland yet still within the Great Barrier Reef Marine Park, the Keppel Islands can be visited from Yeppoon.

While the coral tends to be slightly less colourful than in the north, the Southern GBR, which has the highest percentage of hard coral cover, is widely regarded to be in better health overall, making for some epic diving and snorkelling. Enjoy manta ray sightings galore at Lady Elliot Island, and plenty of turtle action around Heron and Lady Musgrave Islands.

Left Divers, SS *Yongala* wreck **Above top** Manta rays, Lady Elliot Island **Above** Coral polyps

Retreat to the
WHITSUNDAYS

44

ISLAND-HOPPING | TROPICAL HIKES | ROCK ART

From living it up at luxury island resorts to slamming down drinks in the backpacker bars of Airlie Beach, there are plenty of ways to 'do' the Whitsundays. A day trip to the mesmerising swirl of powder-white sand and turquoise water known as Whitehaven Beach is obligatory. But there's plenty more to do. Here's a taste.

P&F PHOTOGRAPHY/ALAMY STOCK PHOTO ©

🗺 How to

Getting here Flights land at Hamilton Island Airport and Whitsunday Coast Airport, 30 minutes from Airlie Beach.

When to go Join in the Airlie Beach and Hamilton Island Race Week yachting festivities in July and August, or beat the crowds during the April–May and November–December shoulder seasons.

Sunset There's only one place to be on Hamilton Island (affectionately known as 'Hamo') as the sun goes down, and that's hilltop bar One Tree Hill.

BEN CALLAHAN/SHUTTERSTOCK ©

DAVID PRUTER/SHUTTERSTOCK ©

Left Sailing in the Whitsundays
Far left top View from Honeyeater Lookout, Airlie Beach **Far left bottom** Sunset, Hamilton Island

Airlie Beach The mainland hub of 'Airlie' is the most affordable base for exploring the 74-island Whitsundays archipelago, part of the Great Barrier Reef Marine Park, with outer-reef and island-hopping excursions available daily. While there's no shortage of backpacker bars and hostels, you'll find family-friendly resorts here, too. For one of the best views in the Whitsundays, make the 8.2km return hike to Honeyeater Lookout; allow three hours.

Hamilton Island hikes The largest inhabited island of the Whitsundays is laced with more than 20km of scenic trails to explore. Leading you to a blissfully secluded cove with a giant timber hammock to laze on, the 5.1km-return Escape Beach Trail is the perfect excuse to stretch your legs. Allow two hours to complete the return hike from the Scenic Trail entrance, or loop back via South East Head, which adds an additional hour of walking.

Island-hopping Bounce between Airlie Beach, Hamilton Island and Daydream Island Resort for a day with Quiksilver Cruises' island-hopper pass, or sign up for one of the many Whitsundays day cruises on offer. More adventurous travellers can join a multi-day sailing adventure, or skipper their own barefoot charter. This is one of the world's only sailing destinations that doesn't require you to have a boating licence – a half-day training session is all you need to set sail.

◎ Hidden Rock Art

The Whitsundays is the traditional home of the Ngaro people, whose connection to the archipelago dates back some 9000 years. Learn more about Ngaro history and culture on an Aboriginal-led day tour from Airlie with Ngaro Indigenous Cultural Tours, which includes a visit to a rock-art site in a hidden corner of the Whitsundays, insights into how the Ngaro saltwater people thrived on the ocean's resources, and a crash course in throwing a traditional fishing spear. The region's first Indigenous guided tour, the memorable experience is run in partnership with local boat-tour and charter company Whitsunday Paradise Explorer.

45

Go Off-Grid on K'GARI

4WD ADVENTURE | FRESHWATER FUN | WILD CAMPING

▬▬▬ Officially renamed in 2021, the K'gari (Fraser Island) World Heritage Area is the world's largest sand island – and one of Australia's greatest adventures. Join an organised tour or tackle the island's 4WD-only trails in your own vehicle in search of waterholes, historical traces, dingoes and more. There are guesthouses and two resorts, but bush and beach camping is a highlight of the K'gari experience.

PETER UNGER/GETTY IMAGES ©

🗺 How to

Getting here Take a ferry or barge from River Heads (south of Hervey Bay) to the western side of K'gari, or the barge from Inskip Point to Hook Point at the island's southern tip.

When to go Fraser is a year-round destination, but the summer months are ideal for swimming.

Hot showers Bring $2 coins to operate the showers at Central Station, Dundubara and Waddy Point Top camping areas.

MATT MUNRO/LONELY PLANET ©

CAM LAIRD/SHUTTERSTOCK ©

Left SS *Maheno* wreck **Far left top** Lake Wabby **Far left bottom** Wild dingo

Swimming spots K'gari's beaches are among the world's most dangerous, but its idyllic freshwater lakes and seaside rock pools make up for it. Chief among them are Lake McKenzie and similarly azure Lake Birrabeen. Strolling the 200m Eli Creek Boardwalk, then floating back downstream, is another K'gari must-do. Just north of Indian Head, the Champagne Pools 'fizz' as seawater spills into the rock pools. And after the 4.1km bushwalk to Lake Wabby, you'll be ready for a dip here, too.

Drives & walks Days on K'gari are best spent exploring by car or on foot. Four scenic inland driving routes offer hours of bumpy fun; allow extra time for bogged-vehicle traffic jams.

Part of the Great Sandy National Park, the island's 40-odd marked walking trails immerse you in surreal landscapes, from tall rainforest to striking sand blows. Look out for cute Krefft's river turtles on the Lake Allom Circuit (1.4km).

Cultural & historical sites The history of the Butchulla people goes back at least 5000 years. Sharp-eyed visitors may spot middens, artefact scatters and scarred trees that bear witness to the first inhabitants' deep and continuing connection to K'gari.

The rusting wreck of the SS *Maheno,* which ran aground in 1935 just north of Eli Creek, is one of K'gari's best-known sights. Learn more about the island's maritime incidents and WWII history on the Sandy Cape Lighthouse Walk (4.8km return) at the island's northern tip.

 Dingo Safety

Around 200 dingoes are thought to roam K'gari in about 30 packs. To ensure a safe encounter (for you and for the sandy-hued wild native dogs), the Queensland National Parks and Wildlife Service advises the following for visitors:

• Never feed dingoes.

• Always stay within arm's reach of children.

• Walk (never run) in groups and carry a stick.

• Camp in fenced areas when possible.

• Keep food stores locked and never store food or food containers in tents.

• Secure all rubbish. With limited garbage bins on the island, it's best to pack it out with you, too.

Practicalities

Right Australian campervan journey

EASY STEPS FROM THE AIRPORT TO THE CITY CENTRE

Located 8km south of central Sydney, Sydney Airport (officially Sydney Kingsford Smith Airport) is Australia's busiest air hub. The international (T1) and domestic (T2 and T3) terminals are 4km apart on either side of the runways. Each has a train station. Melbourne and Brisbane Airports are also major international gateways.

AT THE AIRPORT

EQROY/SHUTTERSTOCK ©

SIM CARDS
Available from the Optus and Vodafone stores in the T1 arrivals hall. Major city supermarkets like Woolworths often have better-value options. If you're travelling through rural Australia, Telstra offers the best coverage; Telstra store locations include the city centre and Bondi Junction.

CURRENCY EXCHANGE
Booths operate in the arrivals hall of Sydney Airport (and other major Australian airports), but airport ATMs offer better rates; choose one belonging to your home bank's global ATM network for fewer fees.

FREE WI-FI Connect to Free SYD Wi-Fi, then follow the prompts. Connectivity is reasonable, but range doesn't reach the Uber pickup areas.

ATMS Located in the arrivals hall; stick to ATMs belonging to major banks (ANZ, Commonwealth Bank, Westpac), not exchange bureaux.

CHARGING STATIONS Found throughout T1, including near baggage-claim belts 6 and 7. Cables are provided for both Android and Apple phones.

ENTRY FORMALITIES

Duty free Limits per incoming passenger include 50 cigarettes and 2.25L of alcohol (for passengers aged 18 and over) and general goods up to the value of $900 ($450 for people aged under 18).

Biosecurity Quarantine regulations are strict, so declare all goods of animal or vegetable origin. Flowers and fresh food (including meats and cheeses) are prohibited.

GETTING TO THE CITY CENTRE

Train Connects the international and domestic terminals to central Sydney (around $20) in 15 minutes. Trains run every six to 22 minutes from 4.22am (4.42am weekends) to around midnight.

Bus + train For a cheaper alternative, bus 420 connects the terminals to nearby Banksia train station, from where regular trains run to Central. Download the TripView app for planning.

Shuttle bus Airport shuttles head to hotels and hostels in the city centre, and some reach surrounding suburbs and beach destinations. There are numerous airport-to-downtown operators, some with desks in the arrivals hall – expect to pay $15 to $25 to the centre.

HOW MUCH FOR A...

train
$20
15 minutes

shuttle bus
from $15
20-30 minutes

taxi
$45-55
20 minutes

Taxi Costs approximately $45 to $55 and takes around 20 minutes. Pickup is from the front of the terminals.

Ride-share Pickup for Uber and Ola is from the Priority Pick-Up zones, located a short walk from both the international and domestic terminals; follow the signs.

Opal Sydney's public-transport network runs on a ticketing system called Opal (opal.com.au). Rechargeable, 'tap-on, tap-off' Opal cards for adults and children are available from WH Smith (international terminal), NewsLink and Relay (domestic terminal), and both airport train stations. Minimum credit load is $10/5 per adult/child ($35 at airport stations).

OTHER POINTS OF ENTRY

Melbourne Airport Australia's second-busiest international gateway, with daily non-stop flights to New Zealand, the Pacific, Asia and the Americas.

Brisbane & other Queensland airports Serves numerous non-stop international flights, as well as an extensive network of flights within Queensland. It also has good ground connections to the Gold Coast and Sunshine Coast. A handful of non-stop international flights also reach Gold Coast, Sunshine Coast and Cairns Airports.

International cruises Dock at one of two terminals in Sydney: the Overseas Passenger Terminal in Circular Quay (right in the city centre) or the less convenient White Bay Cruise Terminal in inner-city Rozelle. The latter is roughly a 5km taxi or Uber ride from central Sydney. On cruise-ship days, Captain Cook Cruises runs ferries between White Bay, Barangaroo and King Street Wharf (Darling Harbour) in the city centre.

In Melbourne, international cruise ships dock at Station Pier, Port Melbourne, a 4km tram, taxi or Uber ride from the city centre. Other international cruise-ship terminals on Australia's East Coast include Brisbane, Cairns, Newcastle and Eden.

TRANSPORT TIPS TO HELP YOU GET AROUND

Australia is huge, so getting from A to B requires some thought. While driving offers the freedom to travel at your own pace and explore more remote areas poorly serviced by trains and buses, the country's affordable internal flights will save you some long travel days when moving between distant locations.

CAR HIRE

Most car-rental companies in Australia require drivers to be over the age of 21; some add a surcharge for drivers under 25. When booking, check if unlimited kilometres are included; it's almost essential in Australia, as extra kilometres can add to your costs considerably.

AUTOMOBILE ASSOCIATIONS

Every state and territory has its own automobile club, among them NSW's NRMA (mynrma.com.au), Victoria's RACV (racv.com.au) and Queensland's RACQ (racq.com. au). All are handy resources for road rules and driving tips, as well as insurance and holiday information.

CAR RENTAL PER DAY

from $50

Petrol approx $1.80/litre

Diesel approx $1.80/litre

DRIVING LICENCES To drive in Australia you'll need to hold a current driving licence issued in English from your home country, or, if the licence isn't in English, you'll also need to carry an International Driving Permit, issued in your home country.

ROOS AHEAD Kangaroos sometimes jump onto country roads, especially at night, dawn and dusk. Avoid driving at these times. If a roo does leap out in front of you, brake in as straight a line as possible to wipe off speed, and only then swerve if safe.

DRIVING ESSENTIALS

Drive on the left; the steering wheel is on the right.

Speed limit: 50km/h or 60km/h in urban areas; 100km/h or 110km/h on highways.

0.05%

Blood-alcohol limit: 0.05% (0% for drivers on a learner's or provisional licence).

Seat belts are mandatory for all passengers; small children must be belted into an approved safety seat.

Give way to the right at intersections and roundabouts.

Respect the rules Road rules are strictly enforced. Red-light and speed cameras are common, and being just a few kilometres over the limit can land you a hefty fine. High-tech cameras can now also detect motorists handling mobile phones while driving, which is illegal and subject to heavy fines. At roadside tram and light-rail stops, always stop behind the tram until the doors have closed and any disembarking passengers are safely off the road.

FLYING Time pressure, combined with the scale of the Australian continent, can make air travel a very convenient option. The country's flight network is extensive, safe and generally competitive. Qantas (qantas.com) is the flag carrier, with Virgin Australia (virginaustralia.com) the nation's other full-service airline, and Rex (rex.com.au) the regional option. Popular low-cost carriers include Jetstar (jetstar.com) and Bonza (flybonza.com).

BUS & TRAIN Buses are handy for budget travellers. Greyhound Australia operates an especially extensive network along the East Coast. Long-distance train travel in Australia is comfortable and affordable but slow, with no high-speed connections.

BICYCLE Cycling around Australia is possible, but distances can be gruelling. In the major cities, kerbside bike lanes and off-road trails are increasingly common; invest in a heavy-duty lock to avoid theft. Bike helmets are compulsory nationwide.

EAST COAST AUSTRALIA GETTING AROUND

KNOW YOUR CARBON FOOTPRINT A domestic flight from Sydney to Melbourne would emit about 245kg of carbon dioxide per passenger. A car would emit around 196kg of carbon dioxide per passenger, while a train would emit about 57kg of carbon dioxide.

There are a number of carbon calculators online. We use Resurgence at resurgence.org/resources/carbon-calculator.html.

ROAD DISTANCE CHART (KMS)

	Wilsons Promontory	Melbourne	Sydney	Newcastle	Byron Bay	Brisbane	Noosa	Bundaberg	Airlie Beach
Melbourne	211								
Sydney	968	879							
Newcastle	1118	1029	170						
Byron Bay	1714	1626	766	618					
Brisbane	1868	1665	924	782	164				
Noosa	2013	1811	1067	919	314	148			
Bundaberg	2105	1903	1265	1123	526	360	239		
Airlie Beach	2588	2385	1871	1729	1263	1097	987	769	
Cairns	3049	2818	2416	2291	1845	1678	1568	1351	619

SAFE TRAVEL

Australia is one of the safest travel destinations in the world. That said, it pays to use common sense and to be aware of the few but real risks you may encounter by the water, in the bush and on city streets.

SWIMMING Hazards include rips, sharks, jellyfish and, in northern Queensland, crocodiles; heed safety signs and swim between the flags where surf lifeguards are on beach patrol. There's also sunburn: wear SPF50+ sunscreen, a broad hat and sunglasses, particularly in the warmer months.

BUSHFIRES Bushfires can be fast moving and unpredictable, especially in spring and summer. Check the fire danger rating, which ranges from Low-Moderate to Catastrophic, for the district you're in. If fires are in your area, pay attention to the news and follow any orders to evacuate. One of the best apps for monitoring wildfires is Australian Fires.

URBAN SAFETY While crime rates are relatively low, avoid walking alone late at night and never leave valuables in a parked car, especially within sight. Keep an eye on your belongings in public places and be cautious if someone offers you a drink in a bar; drink spiking is not unheard of, especially for women.

INSURANCE
Essential for all travellers. Some policies specifically exclude activities such as scuba diving, skiing and even bushwalking. Make sure the policy you choose fully covers you for your planned activities and interests.

Snakes You're very unlikely to encounter snakes in the city. In bushland, urban or rural, stick to trails and avoid long grass. If you see a snake, leave it alone. If bitten, call an ambulance.

OLGA KASHUBIN/SHUTTERSTOCK ©

GALEXIA/SHUTTERSTOCK ©

Bushwalking Always choose a trail within your realm of fitness and experience, and check with local authorities for weather and track updates. Also, tell someone where you are going and when you will be back.

HITCH-HIKING
Despite the general friendliness of Australians, hitching a ride is dangerous and never recommended, whether you're in the city or the country. This applies to both solo travellers and those travelling in pairs.

QUICK TIPS TO HELP YOU MANAGE YOUR MONEY

CREDIT CARDS Visa and MasterCard are widely accepted for accommodation, activities, meals and drinks, and are also essential when renting a car. Contactless payment is the norm, and Apple Pay and Google Pay are also increasingly popular. Credit cards can be used for cash advances at ATMs and banks, but transaction charges apply. Diners Club and American Express (Amex) are not as widely accepted.

CURRENCY

Australian dollar

HOW MUCH FOR A...

flat white
$4.50

pint of craft beer
$12

cafe lunch for two
$50

MONEY CHANGERS Foreign currency can be changed at most Australian banks and licensed money changers like Travelex, but the exchange rate for cash withdrawals from an ATM will always be superior.

ATMS & EFTPOS
ATMs are widespread throughout Australia, including in smaller towns. Eftpos terminals – usually offering contactless transactions – are ubiquitous at retailers and hospitality venues and used for even very small transactions.

BARGAINING
Bargaining or haggling is not common practice and generally only acceptable at market stalls, garage sales and in online communities such as Gumtree or Facebook Marketplace. If bargaining, keep it polite and good-humoured.

TAXES & REFUNDS A flat 10% goods and services tax (GST) is applied to most items and experiences for sale and is included in the price quoted. If you purchase goods with a total minimum value of $300 from any one supplier no more than 60 days before you leave Australia, you are entitled to a refund of any GST paid under the Tourist Refund Scheme (TRS). For details, search TRS on the Australian Border Force website (abf.gov.au).

CHEAPER TRAVEL
In major cities, using an electronic, rechargeable transport card is often cheaper than buying single-trip tickets.

PAYING THE BILL
While most cafes have table service, it's common to pay at the counter when you leave. You may also need to order at the counter.

TIPPING
While tipping is not obligatory in Australia, many locals leave a modest tip (usually around 10% of the total bill) at restaurants where service has been exceptional. At cafes with great table service, leave the change or tip a dollar or two. In taxis, round up the fare to the nearest dollar.

POSITIVE-IMPACT TRAVEL

Tips to leave a lighter footprint, support local and have a positive impact on local communities.

ON THE ROAD

Report injured wildlife If you come across an injured native animal, contact the relevant state's wildlife rescue organisation. For more information, see wires.org.au (New South Wales), wildlife.vic.gov.au (Victoria) or wrq.org.au (Queensland).

Consider renting an electric vehicle Hertz offers a small range of hybrid rental vehicles. Australian-owned car-sharing company Evee (evee.com.au) lets private car owners rent out their Teslas in various locations across the country.

Grey water If you're travelling in a campervan or caravan, make your grey water more environmentally friendly by choosing natural, plant-based soaps and detergents, dry-wiping plates and cutlery with paper towels before washing up, and pouring vinegar and baking soda down drains to clean them. Also, empty your grey-water tanks regularly.

Choose reusable bags, cups and cutlery These make a handy ecofriendly travel kit.

ASHLEY WHITWORTH/SHUTTERSTOCK ©

GIVE BACK

Save koalas affected by fires, deforestation and disease by donating to the Australia Koala Foundation (savethekoala.com) or the World Wildlife Fund (wwf.org.au).

Plant a tree and help regenerate degraded land by donating to not-for-profit organisations like Carbon Positive Australia (carbon positiveaustralia.org.au) and ReForest Now (reforestnow.org.au).

Volunteer a few hours of your time to an Australian Conservation Foundation (acf.org.au) or Conservation Volunteers Australia (conservationvolunteers.com.au) project, which range from planting and weeding to beach-litter clean-ups.

Eat and shop at places that support and empower local communities and the disadvantaged, such as Streat (streat.com.au) and the Social Studio (thesocialstudio.org) in Melbourne, and Heart Cafe (heartcafe.com.au) and Song Kitchen (songkitchen.com.au) in Sydney.

DOS & DON'TS

Do experience an Indigenous perspective by seeking out Aboriginal-owned tours and cultural experiences.

Don't photograph Aboriginal ceremonies and sites of significance without permission.

Don't throw cigarette butts onto the street or in the landscape; it's illegal and can cause bushfires.

Don't cuddle a koala in Victoria or NSW; it's illegal.

LEAVE A SMALL FOOTPRINT

Spend more time in fewer destinations. Not only will you shrink your footprint, you'll form deeper connections and memories in the place you're in.

Research neighbourhoods in large cities and base yourself in one with good transport links and/or within walking distance of places that interest you.

Book tour operators known for their green credentials. Many are listed at Eco Tourism Australia (ecotourism.org.au).

Bring your own reusable cup to cafes. You'll be saving resources and, in many cases, enjoying a small discount.

GLEN BERLIN/SHUTTERSTOCK ©

SUPPORT LOCAL

Feast sustainably by visiting local farmers markets (farmersmarkets.org.au), organic and biodynamic wineries (grenum.com), and eateries that champion local, seasonal produce and sustainably sourced coffee.

Support businesses that are small and independent over large chains, whether Australian or international.

Buy souvenirs made by local artisans. When buying Aboriginal art, ensure that you are buying authentic items that support the artist and Indigenous communities (indigenousartcode.org).

EAST COAST AUSTRALIA RESPONSIBLE TRAVEL

CLIMATE CHANGE & TRAVEL

It's impossible to ignore the impact we have when travelling, and the importance of making changes where we can. Lonely Planet urges all travellers to engage with their travel carbon footprint. There are many carbon calculators online that allow travellers to estimate the carbon emissions generated by their journey; try resurgence.org/resources/carbon-calculator.html. Many airlines and booking sites offer travellers the option of offsetting the impact of greenhouse gas emissions by contributing to climate-friendly initiatives around the world. We continue to offset the carbon footprint of all Lonely Planet staff travel, while recognising this is a mitigation more than a solution.

RESOURCES

ecotourism.org.au
visitmelbourne.com
queensland.com
parksaustralia.gov.au
australiangeographic.com.au

UNIQUE & LOCAL WAYS TO STAY

From lo-fi camping by wild ocean beaches to living it up in art-crammed, inner-city boutique hotels, Australia's slumber options offer a gamut of experiences. Disconnect from the world in a designer eco cabin, realign your chakras at a holistic spa retreat, or hire a campervan and hit the highway for an epic road trip along Australia's dazzling eastern shores.

HOW MUCH FOR A...

basic campsite
$40

dorm bed
$25

tiny house
$300

TARAS VYSHNYA/SHUTTERSTOCK ©

CAMPERVAN CRUISING

Spectacular scenery and well-maintained roads make Australia prime road-trip territory. If time is on your side, hiring a campervan offers maximum independence. Private holiday-park chains like G'day Parks (gdayparks.com.au) and Big4 (big4.com.au) have locations across Australia, and most are well equipped with family-friendly perks like swimming pools, playgrounds and laundry facilities. If you plan on numerous stops, consider joining one of the chains, which offer member discounts. Bookings for popular national-park camping spots are often handled online by state departments, so plan ahead.

ART HOTELS

The closest thing to a gallery sleepover, art hotels lure with their caches of striking contemporary art. Among them are the Art Series (artseries hotels.com.au) suite of properties: midrange hotels in Melbourne, Brisbane and Adelaide named for (and featuring the work of) a particular modern Australian artist. Free collection tours are offered to guests.

ELISE HASSEY ©

SPA RETREATS

If the budget allows, retreat to one of Australia's seductive spa resorts, where luxurious digs, holistic treatments and sustainable dining are set in lush surrounds. Top choices include Gaia (gaiaretreat.com.au) near Byron Bay and Daintree Eco Lodge (pictured left; daintree-ecolodge.com.au) in Far North Queensland.

TINY HOUSES

To unplug sustainably and fully immerse yourself in Australia's natural beauty, consider spending a few nights in a 'tiny house'. Also known as wilderness or eco cabins, these pocket-size holiday abodes are often set in a secluded corner of a farm or private land. Depending on the cabin, you might find yourself based beside a gurgling river, overlooking mountain ranges or the ocean, or within a stone's throw of a photogenic vineyard.

While these tiny houses may be off the grid, there's nothing rudimentary about many of them. Queen- or king-size beds and kitchen facilities are standard, along with higher-end compostable toilets and bathrooms with (hot) showers. Many also come with a firepit, while others crank up the luxe factor with a sauna, an outdoor bath or edibles from local artisan producers and winemakers.

For standout options, check out Unyoked (unyoked.co), Cabn (pictured left; cabn.life), Shacky (shacky.com), In2TheWild (into thewildescapes.com) and Salty Cabins (saltycabins.com), which together cover destinations across eastern and southern Australia. Just remember to book well ahead: word is out and these petite sanctuaries are a big hit with frazzled city slickers.

BOOKING

Booking accommodation in advance is highly recommended, especially for beach destinations during the Australian summer (December to February), at Easter and over long weekends. Booking ahead is also recommended during winter (June to August) in popular Queensland destinations like the Gold Coast, the Sunshine Coast, the Whitsundays and Port Douglas, when holidaymakers from the southern states head north.

Lonely Planet (lonelyplanet.com/australia/hotels) Find independent reviews and recommendations on the best places to stay, and book them online.

Airbnb (airbnb.com) Wide range of options, from city apartments to beach houses.

Green Getaways (greengetaways.com.au) Beautifully curated selection of stylish, ecofriendly accommodation across Australia.

Great Small Hotels (greatsmallhotels.com) Boutique hotels, inns and resorts.

Luxury Lodges of Australia (luxurylodgesofaustralia.com.au) High-end accommodation, often with a focus on gourmet dining and natural beauty.

Hostelworld (hostelworldgroup.com) Find and book hostels across the country.

G'day Parks (gdayparks.com.au) Caravan and holiday parks throughout Australia.

CAMPING APPS

Camps Australia Wide (camps australiawide. com) has a handy app with maps and information. Other useful resources for campers include Go Camping (gocamping australia.com) and Hipcamp (hipcamp.com).

ESSENTIAL NUTS & BOLTS

BYO

Bring your own (BYO) drinks to a barbecue, and ask whether you should bring a plate (a dish or salad) to share.

SHOUTING

Shouting (buying a round of drinks) is common when out drinking with friends. If someone shouts you, shout them back.

SMOKING

Smoking is banned in most indoor public spaces and some outdoor spaces where crowds congregate.

FAST FACTS

Time Zone
GMT+10

Country Code
+61

Electricity
230V/
50Hz

GOOD TO KNOW

Stand on the left on escalators and overtake on the right. Also, stay on the left when using stairs and footpaths.

All visitors to Australia need a valid visa to enter the country (immi.homeaffairs.gov.au).

If there's a queue, respect it and apologise if you accidentally cut in.

In case of emergency, dial 000 (police, fire and ambulance).

The legal drinking age in Australia is 18; public drinking laws vary between states.

ACCESSIBLE TRAVEL

Key attractions, including some national parks, commonly provide access for those with limited mobility. Numerous places also address visual or aural impairments; see wheeleasy.org.

Hotels commonly have lifts, ramps and rooms with accessible bathrooms; see accessibleaccommodation.com.

Public transport in major cities and towns is usually wheelchair accessible, though some stations and stops are not.

Major taxi companies offer WAV (wheelchair-accessible vehicles); request ahead.

Tour operators with vehicles catering to mobility-impaired travellers operate from most capital cities.

Accessible dining can vary significantly. It's always best to call in advance.

Useful resources include deafaustralia. org.au, visionaustralia.org, ideas.org.au and scia.org.au.

PUNCTUALITY

If you're running more than 10 minutes late to an appointment, text or call ahead to apologise.

GARÇON!

Don't wave or shout to call your waiter. Wait to make eye contact and simply raise your hand.

CHRISTMAS CLOSURES

Many businesses close or reduce their trading hours from Christmas to the second week of January.

FAMILY TRAVEL

Public transport is usually free for children aged under four or five. Older children usually pay half the adult fare.

Admission to some museums and galleries is free. Most paid attractions offer reduced-price tickets for kids.

Hotels can usually provide cots, with notice. Some boutique B&Bs and resorts do not welcome children.

Cafes, pizzerias and casual restaurants are child-friendly. Fine-dining restaurants usually discourage bringing babies or small kids.

Breastfeeding in public is widely accepted.

GOOD MANNERS

Australians are relatively casual and not especially big on formalities. Moderate swearing is common among friends and not always considered rude. Not saying 'please' and 'thank you' is considered rude. So too are intrusive questions about a person's age, weight or income.

GREETINGS

Despite the stereotypes, most Australians do not speak like Mick Dundee or the Crocodile Hunter (especially in urban areas). The most common greeting among locals is 'Hi', 'Hello' or 'Hey'. A friendly 'G'day' is fine but less common than you may think.

HOLLI/SHUTTERSTOCK ©

LGBTIQ+ TRAVELLERS

Homosexuality is legal, and same-sex marriages are legally recognised in Australia.

Australians are generally open-minded, but you may experience some suspicion or hostility in more conservative neighbourhoods or regions. Inner Sydney and Melbourne have especially vibrant gay scenes.

Major events include the Sydney Gay and Lesbian Mardi Gras, and Melbourne's Midsumma Festival and Queer Film Festival.

Online resources include Visit Gay Australia (visitgay australia.com.au), which lists a number of LGBTIQ+ businesses across the country.

Index

'Consider this fair warning: the wild parrots at O'Reilly's Rainforest Retreat will land on your head – and they may leave behind a souvenir.'

JESSICA WYNNE LOCKHART

'I'm calling it: Bundaberg is one of the most underrated destinations on the Queensland coast. From farm gates to reef adventures, there's no shortage of things to do.'

SARAH REID

'My mind still boggles at the tale of an escaped crocodile that once roamed the basement of Melbourne's Manchester Unity Building.'

CRISTIAN BONETTO

'Researching the South Coast gold rush inspired me to resume my childhood gold panning. I've found a whole gram of gold!'

CAOIMHE HANRAHAN-LAWRENCE

'Encountering two koalas fighting in the middle of the Otways was definitely the most unexpected moment of the trip!'

TRENT HOLDEN

THIS BOOK

Design development
Lauren Egan, Tina García, Fergal Condon

Content development
Anne Mason

Cartography development
Wayne Murphy, Katerina Pavkova

Production development
Mario D'Arco, Dan Moore, Sandie Kestell, Virginia Moreno, Juan Winata

Series development leadership
Liz Heynes, Darren O'Connell, Piers Pickard, Chris Zeiher

Commissioning editor
Daniel Bolger

Product editor
Saralinda Turner

Cartographers
Corey Hutchison, Rachel Imeson

Book designer
Virginia Moreno

Assisting editors
James Appleton, Sarah Bailey, Nigel Chin

Cover researcher
Kat Marsh

Thanks Gwen Cotter, Amy Lynch, Darren O'Connell, Charlotte Orr, John Taufa

MEISTER PHOTOS/SHUTTERSTOCK ©